'How to be a Change Superhero is practitioners who wish to succeed invaluably pragmatic guide to mana... successful change – and we all know how hard that is! Lucinda brings a fresh and pragmatic approach to the subject. While she reveals learnings from her favourite academics and experts, and covers the process and structure of change, the main value of this excellent book is how it covers the critical subject of people – how to motivate, how to communicate, how to listen, how to empathise, how to corroborate to deliver the change you need. I loved it!'

Campbell Macpherson, author of *The Change Catalyst* (2017), 2018 Business Book of the Year, British Business Book Awards

'How to be a Change Superhero is a wonderfully pragmatic guide for anyone involved in organizational or business change. The book covers the role of the individual in change, giving a practical insight into how people react and invariably providing grounded, realistic advice on how best to deal with the inevitable tricky reactions that tend to happen as people interact. There are a lot of books covering the theory of change, but this is a rare foray into a more practical approach, and an excellent one at that. Whilst there is no shortage of real-life examples dropped in there is also coverage of some of the classic theories in this space, always explained in an accessible fashion.'

David D'Souza, Membership Director of the CIPD; Fellow of the Learning Performance Institute, the Centre for Evidence-Based Management

'Change happens. We all know it and we're either causing change, or we're being affected by it. This is true in life and especially in organizations. Lucinda Carney takes the reality of organizational change and gives it definition and form so that we can lead change instead of being its victim. This book is solid from its first word until its last. You need to have a copy of this book sitting at the ready so that you can be the Change Superhero you were meant to be!'

Steve Browne, author of *HR On Purpose: Developing Deliberate People Passion* (2017)

'The only constant is change, as every Leader and HR professional knows. But it's not always an easy process and this book gives you everything you need and much more to be a highly effective catalyst for change and make lasting organisational improvements. Lead the change you seek and do it in an informed and effective manner as a fully charged Change Superhero.'

Ruth Cornish, CEO, Amelore Consulting

'Change can be painful – we've all had it thrust upon us at some point or have been on the receiving end of a badly implemented change management process. Drawing on her years of experience in the field of change, Lucinda has demystified what is required for successful change to happen. Bursting at the seams with theories and concepts made relevant and digestible, Lucinda's engaging tone and pace means that you whizz through each chapter, absorbing practical and realistic advice as you go. This is going to be in the well-thumbed and highlighted section of my bookcase!'

Jo Keeler, Managing Partner, Belbin

HOW TO BE
A
CHANGE
SUPERHERO

*The business toolkit to help you to 'do'
change better*

LUCINDA CARNEY

First published in Great Britain by Practical Inspiration Publishing, 2020

ISBN   9781788601603   (print)
       9781788601597   (epub)
       9781788601580   (mobi)

Practical Inspiration
PUBLISHING

Contents

Acknowledgements

Well, all I can say is that this has been a long time coming. I had the idea for this book almost ten years ago but it took the ten-day business book proposal challenge by Alison Jones at Practical Inspiration Publishing to get it out of my head and onto the page. Thank you to Michelle Parry-Slater for signposting me to Alison in the first place; she is brilliant.

Being the CEO of a software business while writing a book is a challenge, so I must first thank my husband and business partner Chris Carney and the whole team at Actus Software who kept everything ticking over brilliantly when my head had to be in the book rather than in the business. Thanks particularly to Gemma Scott, who has had the joy of editing various aspects of my business writing and politely calls me out when I don't make sense. Huge thanks also to my neighbour and good friend Will Cameron, who stepped in at the final hour when I had bitten off more than I could chew regarding editing the manuscript – even if he has edited out all the exclamation marks except this one!

Much of my early experience around managing change came from my internal learning and organizational development roles at Siemens and Pfizer. Since 2009 this has multiplied through my consultancy work at Advance Change Ltd (which also trades as Actus). This has given me access to hundreds of public, private and not-for-profit organizations with countless different People Professionals (Change Superheroes) dealing with their own cultural challenges. Thank you to everyone who has contributed with their experiences and challenges, which have taught me so much and hopefully enriched this book for others by sharing real examples.

My teenage children Emma and Sammy should be recognized for being so positive and supportive as well as patient with the 'Mummy has to write her book now' interruptions to this year's summer holiday and countless weekends. The fact that they are vaguely impressed that I have written and published a book means a lot to me. Unfortunately, neither of my parents are alive to see this but my father Dr David Harley was a huge book lover and I would hope that seeing his daughter make it into print would also have made him very proud.

I'm a huge pragmatist so I have tried to keep this book as accessible and practical as possible. With this in mind, at the end of each chapter there is a short case study designed to illustrate some of the points made within that chapter. I have kept them anonymous to protect the innocent; however, I would like to extend sincere thanks to the following contributors: Kim Bradford, Willorna Brock, Teresa Cameron, Karen Gill, Steve Graham, Sophie Haylock, Cat Hase, Steve Jones, Craig Marshall, Ali Nutley, Jennifer Scherler and Fran Trousdale. Thank you to Sheila Lardner, a long-time training colleague and friend, for the blue-bag-and-potatoes analogy and other inspiration, and to Grant Whiteing for the illustrations.

Finally, thanks to you, the reader, for picking this book out of all the others that you could have chosen. I truly hope that you find it practical and inspiring.

About the author

Lucinda Carney is a chartered psychologist with many years of corporate experience as a People Professional (HR and Learning and Development). She personally initiated and drove many cultural change initiatives within organizations as an internal Change Agent and has supported countless more through her consultancy firm Advance Change Ltd.

As CEO of Actus Software (www.actus.co.uk) she has worked extensively across the private, public and not-for-profit sectors supporting clients with culture change, leadership and management skills and was recognized as the Everywoman in Technology Entrepreneur of the Year in 2016.

Lucinda is an experienced trainer, facilitator, speaker and coach with accreditations in many psychological tools. She has always been fascinated by 'what makes people tick' and believes strongly that understanding and valuing individual differences can reduce conflict and engender collaboration during change. She is passionate about making a difference to others and has developed a suite of training courses and valuable free materials to support budding Change Superheroes, which can be downloaded via the website www.changesuperhero.com.

She hosts the weekly podcast The HR Uprising, which went to the number-one spot in the iTunes business charts in the week of launch and has built a loyal and growing fan base with other People Professionals as well as those in broader business roles. You can access the back catalogue of podcasts, including a number that relate to change, at www.hruprising.com. Lucinda can be contacted on LinkedIn, on Twitter @lucindacarney or email lucinda@actus.co.uk.

Lucinda lives in Hertfordshire, UK and is married to Chris with two children, Emma and Sammy, two dogs, two cats and a bearded dragon. She is a keen netballer and is actively involved in the local community within the village of Redbourn.

Introduction

When was the last time you experienced change at work – did you feel it was being *done* to you, or perhaps you were involved in trying to communicate or deliver it? Did the change achieve the promised results, or did it fizzle out? How effectively was it managed? Did it leave people energized, puzzled or cynical?

The reality is that change has become the new normal, yet many changes are still poorly planned, communicated or implemented. It is rare for us to hear that managers or employees have been trained in how to deliver or react to change. Even people with transformation or change in their job title are often poorly prepared for the complex requirements of managing change well. Ultimately, poorly managed change results in reduced business outcomes and can leave people emotionally damaged by the experience. So, isn't it time to 'do change' better?

How to be a Change Superhero is aimed at anyone who wants to feel better equipped to manage, deliver or respond to change in the workplace. We will explore the skills and traits (Superpowers) that can be helpful when involved in change and consider how we can develop these. We will also consider the human and cultural responses to change (Heroes and Villains) that can make change feel smooth or bumpy. Finally, we will explore how to bring this all together into a change 'Master Plan' that will allow you to utilize the strengths of a team (your Change League) and understand clearly how to plan and deliver large-scale change successfully.

This book is primarily aimed at those involved in organizational or business change and I will use these terms interchangeably. That said, several chapters will also be relevant to those of us experiencing personal change too. Don't worry if you are already tiring of the Superhero analogies; they are here to lighten the topic and make the book accessible to all. I replace the term Change Superhero with the more commonly used expression Change Agent in many places. Ultimately, this book should be relevant to anyone who is involved in designing or implementing organizational change, which is most of us nowadays. It is my hope that you will find this book easy to read, yet highly applicable and practical whatever your level of experience. I have tried to strike a balance between theory, personal examples and practical tools that you can pick up and run with.

The book is divided into three parts; the first is about the individual skills or Superpowers that we need to develop for us to become potential Change Superheroes. The second focuses on 'Change Challenges'; this includes the people who resist and challenge change, making your life harder, as well as specific hurdles that we come across during change, which are often cultural or structural. Finally, the third part is themed 'Building a Change Master Plan' and is about working with others to deliver large-scale change successfully. Each chapter will feature a summary of key takeaways, a real-life case study to illustrate some of the points made in that chapter and, where applicable, useful tools and resources that you can download for free from our website, which can be accessed at www.changesuperhero.com.

PART I

The five Superpowers of a Change Superhero

People don't resist change. They resist being changed.
Peter Senge

Do you sometimes feel that you need to possess Superpowers to deliver change in your organization? If you felt like a Change Superhero, how much easier would it be to deliver results both human and organizational? I had some reservations about using this analogy at first because of the risk of suggesting that we simply swoop in, deliver a bit of change and then disappear, leaving the hard work of actually 'doing change' still to be done. The reverse is intended because this breed of Change Superhero sticks around to see the job through. True Change Superheroes instinctively understand the Peter Senge quote above: that people don't resist change for the sake of it – they resist having change 'done' to them. However, the reality is that change needs to be 'done' in organizations worldwide, daily; that's why I use the term 'do' change differently as our guiding principle.

Change Superheroes are brave and prepared to stand up and be counted. They are also humble with genuine depth of character; they understand and are true to their values and are committed to getting the job done – properly. This means that they have an armoury of additional skills, such as emotional intelligence, the ability to both lead and follow, as well as a flexibility of communication style that can be adapted to the needs of the audience or situation.

The reality is that few of us are born with all of these natural strengths or 'Superpowers' and it's highly unlikely that we have our own 'Justice League' to call upon to counteract our natural blind spots or development areas. It is down to us to develop a range of skills and some will come more easily to us than others. This means that we need to start with self-awareness about our natural strengths and preferences. Then we need to factor in our blind spots and have strategies to either overcome these or bring others in to support. It is all about flexibility and adapting our approach to the audience or environment, and any of us can do it if we try.

The first part of this book outlines the five Superpowers of a Change Superhero and how we can develop and master these, building a strong personal foundation to deliver sustainable business change. We start with courage, which is about emotional intelligence: understanding ourselves before trying to lead others. Connecting with strategy is our second 'Superpower', which is about our ability to create a vision and rationale for change that overcomes resistance and inspires people to follow. Once people understand the vision, they may still require corroboration or evidence that the change is worthwhile to them or people that they care about. These first three Superpowers are about the Change Agent personally and these need to be mastered or clarified before we interact with others. Chapters 4 and 5 are about communication and collaboration respectively, which involve other people, because change cannot be achieved in a vacuum. Ideas on how to communicate effectively to build a successful league of like-minded Change Agents and the techniques for close collaboration will close out the first part of this book. Everyone is different and some of us will find it easier to demonstrate one Change Superpower over another. You can download our simple 'Five Superpowers of a Change Superhero' quiz at www.changesuperhero.com to analyze your own natural strengths and get tips on how to develop others.

CHAPTER 1

Courage

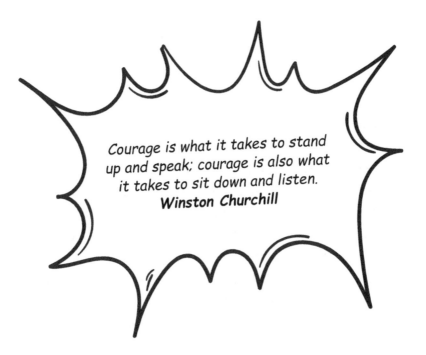

Courage is what it takes to stand up and speak; courage is also what it takes to sit down and listen.
Winston Churchill

Why do we start with courage? Well for me this is the foundation of any successful Change Agent's skillset, as delivering change is rarely easy. As Winston Churchill's quotation suggests, courage doesn't have to be just on the battlefield; it starts with our psychology, knowing when to speak and when to listen. We need to develop the courage to understand and lead ourselves psychologically before being ready to lead others. As budding Change Agents, we need to be prepared to develop psychological courage, facing our fears a bit like the Lion in *The Wizard of Oz*. We may have to 'stand up and be counted' against the tide of opinion or find ourselves in conflict with others. We might find ourselves in a situation where we are asked to lead a project on behalf of the business yet find that some of the key opposition comes from the most senior people in the organization. There is no doubt that we need courage to politely challenge the resistance of those senior to us, given that it could be seen to be career-limiting.

This chapter is fundamentally about psychological courage. First, we will explore the challenge of standing up to senior colleagues before going on to explore the broader subject of self-awareness and emotional intelligence. To be true Change Superheroes we need to be courageous enough to get to know and master our own emotions and behaviours. This chapter starts to show us how to do this. It will give us the foundation to understand how to connect with the corporate strategy and appreciate when and how to engage in persuasion, communication and collaboration – all key Superpowers that our Change Superheroes will need to deploy for success.

'Well that's never going to work': challenging resistance from senior colleagues

My personal experience of needing to summon up courage was when I was involved in delivering an organizational change programme requiring the whole business to get on board. I had been tasked with driving the project by the board, with the full support of the CEO and most board members. This should have been enough to get the project signed off and sponsored. However, I knew that the director of operations was cynical about the potential benefits of the change within his area, which made up a third of the business. My concern was that this individual would undermine the initiative covertly. He was senior to me and I had never found him easy to get on with, so as you can imagine I wasn't enthusiastic about having to deal with him personally. However, I also knew that it was unlikely that the project would succeed fully if we didn't have his support.

So, I summoned up my courage and booked a one-to-one meeting with him. In this meeting I shared the vision for the project and asked for his feedback. I listened to his opinion, acknowledged any concerns and made a few small tweaks to the proposal in line with his feedback. What sticks in my mind is how minor most of his suggested changes were. Most notable was a request to simply change the direction of an arrow on an image of the overall vision. It didn't significantly change the vision or the meaning, but that was all it took to get his buy-in. A couple of weeks later, I presented the overall proposal for final board approval and was able to reference his adjustments, displaying his endorsement, which paved the way to a straightforward board sign-off.

This individual was known to be difficult and cynical but, whatever my opinion about his motives, he may still have had genuine concerns. By summoning up the courage to listen to his concerns I was able to make some minor adjustments and get his support. It was almost as if he didn't actually have any real objections but just wanted to be consulted (I have subsequently found that this is surprisingly common). So, it was important for me to sit down on a personal level with him to ensure that he wouldn't undermine the project. If I'm honest, I wouldn't say he was ever a champion, but he didn't become a blocker either.

So, to be an effective Change Agent we need to have the courage to talk to people on a personal level, whatever their level of seniority. We can't be intimidated by status because sponsors can make or break a change initiative, sometimes unintentionally. I once witnessed this during an important technology change programme for a small media firm. It had been a significant investment and the CEO was taking part in the system training along with a range of delegates from all over his business. He wasn't particularly technical and suddenly blurted out: 'Well, that's never going to work!'

I don't think he realized the extent to which his throwaway comment potentially undermined the entire investment and programme success. We often hear that technology investments fail due to people issues and it is easy to see how easily this can happen if role models who should be sponsoring a programme are overheard making comments that undermine it. Of course, we must remember that they are human too and will also have natural responses to any change. A courageous Change Agent needs to pre-empt this from happening, particularly with key sponsors or other highly visible or influential individuals. This may mean personally making contact at an early stage to explain the change or agreeing the key messages and gaining explicit commitment for their reinforcement. Having gained explicit commitment from someone to support the messages makes it far easier for us to politely provide feedback if they then behave differently. Everyone is human, but it still takes Superhero levels of courage and subtlety to challenge those senior to us in a positive fashion.

Throughout this book, we will consider the wide variety of ways in which people view the world and communicate, which means that one style will never suit everyone or every purpose. This provides us, as budding Change Superheroes, with the almost paradoxical requirement to learn to wear multiple hats without being seen to be 'faking it'. This requires us to be highly self-aware and flexible. You might even say that we need to be our own 'Change League', all wrapped up within one Superhero cape. We will need to draw on the skills of others later in the process, but psychological courage, personal leadership and flexibility are the first key skills for us to hone.

By psychological courage, I mean being brave enough to really understand our own motivations and behaviours and to take responsibility for how they impact on others. This is quite different from physical courage. As we improve our self-awareness, we have more choices about how we behave making us more flexible. If we want to deliver change successfully, we need to be flexible enough to both lead and follow. We may have to be diplomatic and challenging, or open yet restrained. This requires high levels of self-awareness and self-control, sometimes referred to as emotional intelligence, which is a great concept for us to use as the basis for understanding how to develop psychological courage.

Emotional intelligence

The term emotional intelligence (EI) is most well known through the work of American psychologist Daniel Goleman (1996). His work identified five different aspects of EI, all of which can be used to underpin this concept of psychological courage when delivering change. These are described as self-awareness; self-control; self-motivation; empathy and social skills.

Self-awareness

This is our own understanding of 'what makes us tick', including what motivates us, our personality and the way in which we typically react to situations or how we come across to others. In the context of this book, it is particularly valuable for us to know how we personally react to change as well as how people react to our typical communication style. An example of self-awareness might be my knowledge that I have a natural tendency to talk quickly. Through feedback, I also understand that this can give the impression to others that I am nervous or excited. This may or may not be a true reflection of my emotions, but what is important is the fact that I know that I can unintentionally negatively portray the message by speaking at my natural pace, whether it is true or not. Clearly, if I am communicating information surrounding a change, appearing to be nervous or excited may well be inappropriate, so I can use this self-awareness and choose to speak more slowly.

In Chapters 7 and 10, we will look at individual differences in terms of personality types and the roles we prefer to play in teams. Separately, in Chapter 4 we will consider motivational differences and how we like to take in and process information. This is not to put ourselves or others into a 'box', but to appreciate our habitual preferences and behaviours and how they may impact on others during change. It also puts us in a stronger position to be able to communicate effectively and be understood by others. This self-awareness, coupled with the courage to exercise self-control in terms of our interactions with others, is a vital attribute of a successful Change Agent.

Self–control

This is sometimes referred to as self-regulation. Essentially, it is about us understanding our natural impulses and personality traits and choosing the most appropriate response for a given situation – as opposed to our automatic one. It may involve self-restraint, perhaps from our default response, or it may be about flexing our behavioural response away from our habitual one. Examples might be empathizing with the views of others rather than blindly defending our case, or challenging the status quo rather than sitting back and waiting.

Self-control is something that can be learned; it is a bit like a muscle that can benefit from exercise. However, we need both self-awareness and motivation if we are to change our habitual behaviours. Understanding that certain behaviours tend to result in negative outcomes may motivate us to exercise more self-control. Another way of motivating ourselves to exercise self-control on demand is by considering what we want as an outcome following a specific interaction. By visualizing the likely outcome of a specific interaction, we give ourselves the opportunity to demonstrate the most appropriate behaviours for the outcomes we prefer. Self-control enables us to make choices that result in better outcomes. We have all probably been told to 'count to ten' before responding when angry. If we use these ten seconds to consider a range of possible responses and the likely outcome of each, then we can select the best response for that situation. The best response is hardly ever our automatic response and usually involves self-control, but it will generate better long-term relationships and results.

Self-motivation

It is common for people with high levels of EI to also have high levels of self-motivation, which can be defined as the ability to determine what needs to be done and to do it without outside influence. People with self-motivation find the need and determination to complete tasks, even under challenging circumstances, without either giving up or needing external encouragement. As Change Agents, we can quite often feel that we are a lone voice having to swim against the tide. Change can be unpopular, and people may also display high levels of resistance or apathy towards change. Therefore, it can take a huge amount of energy and persistence to continue pushing the change through when the majority are blocking or resisting it. Those with high levels of self-motivation and drive are going to be better at seeing any change through to completion, including overcoming the many obstacles and setbacks that may be encountered along the way. The best way to develop self-motivation is through creating a clear vision and then setting and keeping small commitments that align with it. It is important to tune into our 'self-talk' to make sure it is staying positive and to reward ourselves for demonstrating self-motivation and self-control, building resilience. We need to learn to be our own cheerleader, especially when things get tough.

Empathy

When we demonstrate that we understand the emotions of others, we are showing empathy. This empathy may be evidenced non-verbally through our body language and facial expressions. We may also vocalize empathy using terms like 'I understand' or verbalizing what we perceive to be the emotion demonstrated by the other person, e.g., 'That sounds frustrating'. We will talk more about this in Chapter 4, on communication. Empathy is particularly important because people go through a predictable range of emotions during change, known as the transition or 'Change Curve', which we explain in detail in Chapter 6. If people get stuck at a particular stage of the Change Curve because they don't feel that their concerns are being heard or addressed satisfactorily, then the entire project may fail.

Our ability to empathize with the emotions of others builds trust and mutual understanding, which in turn will help us to deliver change. You could say that we need to have the courage to show that we care by demonstrating empathy.

Social skills

The final EI attribute defined by Goleman is having good social skills. This is our ability to interact positively and build relationships with others. It is in many ways a culmination of the four other aspects of EI, with a healthy dose of communication skills thrown in. Essentially, EI starts with being able to understand our own emotions (self-awareness), then learning to manage them (self-control) and using them to set and achieve goals (self-motivation). Once we can understand and manage ourselves then we can start to understand the emotions and feelings of others (empathy) and finally choose the best communication style and behaviours to influence them or to work together positively (social skills).

The challenge is often about demonstrating the right combination of behaviours for the right social situation in order to create the impression that we want. This can be easier said than done, but is particularly important during change because we really need to take people with us. In other words, we need to be able to lead the change and this may require us influencing others to follow.

Transformational leadership

It takes courage and commitment for us to harness our own natural attributes and flex them to achieve the best outcome in any given situation. EI takes us on the journey from leading ourselves to leading others, and it would be reasonable to describe someone who is effective at leading others through change as being a 'transformational leader'. This is supported by academic research suggesting that transformational leaders tend to have high levels of EI (Ugoani, Amu & Kalu, 2015). However, the term transformational leadership, rather like EI, can sometimes be guilty of falling into the category of leadership jargon or buzzwords. Therefore, we may ask: what do we mean by transformational leadership and why is it so important in relation to change?

Transformational leadership as a concept was introduced by leadership expert and presidential biographer James MacGregor Burns (2003) and further developed by researcher Bernard M. Bass (2005). Essentially, it is all about those in leadership positions providing the personal touch and building trust, which in turn inspires others to follow. This may seem to be fairly commonsensical now that we operate in flatter structures, but in the 1970s business was more hierarchical and demonstrating a personal touch may have seemed more exceptional.

We will go on in future chapters to talk about the practicalities of change, how we can provide evidence for change and communicate in ways that are more likely to influence others to want to change. However, it is important to remember that these can be considered mere tactics if they are not coupled with the personal integrity of a naturally transformational leader. This is a key point for us to remember as budding Change Superheroes: none of this is about pretending to 'be' something in order to manipulate others to change. We may get away with that once, but definitely not in the long run. We need to start by leading ourselves, by developing our emotional intelligence personally and behaving consistently in line with our values and doing what we say we will. This consistency builds trust, which makes people choose to follow us. Therefore, we could imagine that being considered a transformational leader is the result of our consistent, courageous efforts to develop our character and behaviour.

As the word 'transformation' suggests, transformational leadership skills are highly desirable when leading change – particularly culture change. They focus on the empowerment, engagement and motivation of individuals as opposed to the counter-point – transactional leadership – which is more about working within the status quo, focusing on management activities like compliance, productivity, structure or hierarchy – in other words, 'doing' or 'implementing' change. As we might expect, research (Herold, Fedor, Caldwell & Liu, 2008) has shown a positive correlation between transformational leadership skills and employee commitment to change or buy-in, which is of course what we are after. This has been further supported by the work of Higgs and Rowland (2011), who found that more facilitating and engaging leadership behaviours were positively related to change success.

However, transactional leadership also has a valid role to play in change, particularly when embedding change, which is often where change fails. A simple way to think about it is that we need to demonstrate transformational leadership skills when dealing with the human aspects of change, and transactional leadership skills when we manage the systems and processes involved in embedding change; both are essential if we want to achieve long-lasting results.

In the same way that we have natural levels of EI that can be developed and enhanced, we also have natural preferences for transformational or transactional leadership styles. So, by having the courage and commitment to work on the five attributes of EI, we are more likely to be effective as transformational leaders and Change Agents – these are key skills for leading others. However, if we also possess great transactional leadership skills, these should also be celebrated.

So, courage in this context is mainly psychological; it is about personal mastery through self-awareness and making wise behavioural choices. This equates to the ability to lead ourselves, which in turn makes us better transformational leaders and better able to lead others. However, there is one final aspect to courage that is also important to cover. Sometimes, it is just as important to have the courage to follow others as it is to lead.

Having the courage to follow

You may have seen the TED Talk by Derek Sivers called 'How To Start A Movement' (2010). It shows a video of a man dancing alone in a field at a music festival. He is waving his arms around and dancing in a crazy fashion, being watched with curiosity by many other seated festival-goers. No doubt, many people would have initially considered him someone to avoid, rather than someone to follow. Nevertheless, he carries on, appearing to be thoroughly enjoying himself without being in the least bit self-conscious. After a while, a second person joins him – 'The First Follower', in Sivers' terms. This First Follower emulates the crazy, unselfconscious dance moves – somehow giving the act credibility. Then a few more followers join in and, before long, more people are dancing the crazy dance than are sitting watching. Suddenly, it seems more uncool to be watching than it is to be part of the crazy dance movement.

Change is all about creating a movement, and every movement needs a first, second and third follower. In Chapter 5 we explain the core skills of collaboration, which we can use to build our own movement. However, the point here is that it takes as much courage to follow someone into the unknown, to back an early change and to give it credibility, as it does to start the change in the first place. Change Superheroes don't mind if they start a movement, or if they are simply the First Follower; delivering the change or creating the movement is their priority. So, to be a Change Superhero, it all starts with psychological courage – and it is up to us whether we choose to develop it or not.

Case study in brief: having the courage to challenge long-established norms

Company info: medical engineering and manufacturing plant; 400 people.

Background: a new managing director (MD) took over an engineering firm and wanted to establish clear values around consistency and fairness. He inherited a legacy company-car scheme that was inconsistently applied. His predecessors had either tried to change it and had met insurmountable resistance or had chosen to turn a blind eye.

Action: the MD felt strongly that it was a matter of personal integrity for him to address this inconsistency as it symbolized his approach to fairness and consistency; this would of course affect whether people trusted him as their leader. He knew that even though it would be painful (he had been warned of the risk of strike or a walk-out), he needed the courage to address this issue where others hadn't in order to set up the right leadership culture for future transformation. Through consultation, he came up with an approach that clearly defined which roles were eligible for company cars. Those who were in roles that were no longer eligible were given a replacement payment over three years that allowed them to transition to their own cars. This provided a consistent platform for the future without unduly disadvantaging those who were directly affected.

Result: there was no walk-out and the employees broadly accepted the change and saw it as fair. Most importantly, they respected the MD for having the courage to address a long-standing area of unfairness. He went on to make other huge changes to the way the plant operated, resulting in it winning many awards and being recognized as highly productive and culturally effective.

Quick recap on courage

- Psychological courage is at the root of being a Change Superhero.
- To deliver change, we cannot be intimidated by seniority.
- Effective change leaders have high levels of emotional intelligence, which can be developed.
- Transformational leadership is key to gaining buy-in from others.
- It is equally important during change to both follow and lead.

Online toolkit

The following free change resources can be downloaded via: www.changesuperhero.com

- The 'Five Superpowers of a Change Superhero' quiz
- The 'Five Superpowers of a Change Superhero' infographic

CHAPTER 2

Connecting with strategy

Good business leaders create a vision, articulate the vision, passionately own the vision, and relentlessly drive it to completion.
Jack Welch

A strategy defines the vision or plan for an organization, designed to help it survive and prosper within a future environment. A strategy can be defined as a concept, a process and an output. In this chapter we are mainly referring to it as a concept that provides people with a reason to change. Jack Welch, ex-CEO of General Electric and business author, explains the importance of communicating a passionate vision, coupled with relentless follow-through, in order to deliver change.

Notice the use of the term 'passionate'. Going through the motions simply won't work when leading others to change; we need to be prepared to get fully 'on the bus' (another Jack Welch term) and have the courage to be the passionate 'First Follower' if we are to convince others to join in.

So, in this chapter we start by gathering the courage to take the lead and show how connecting with the strategy helps to take others with us. We will start to see some of the thinking that has already been done to allow people to share a compelling vision and see its connection to change. We will examine how the need for change can be analyzed and then show the best way to set goals to achieve your change ambitions. Sometimes people may not want to change, but if they can see the connection between the change and an overall strategy or goal that they consider to be of value, then they are better able to buy in to the change.

The Change Equation

Linking to strategy often requires us to tell a story, which may be about exciting positives or may also be about avoiding potential negatives. Richard Beckhard and Reuben Harris wrote about a formula for change known as the Change Equation in their book *Organizational Transitions: Managing Complex Change* (Beckhard & Harris, 1987). This change formula is a useful model to consider here, as we can use it as a structure around which to build our story.

$$C = [ABD] > X$$

Where C = making it happen, A = level of dissatisfaction with the status quo, B = desirability of the proposed change or end state, D = practicality of the change (knowledge of the next practical step, minimal risk and disruption) and X = cost of change.

According to this formula, there are three key factors to consider during change. First, the rationale for change must be clearly laid out, linking to the strategy. This may be about explaining the current or future problems associated with the status quo, making the need to change seem inevitable. Second, the end goal or vision for the change needs to be communicated in an appealing way, focusing on the benefits of the change – both organizational and personal. Third, the initiative must appear to be well thought-through and practical, reducing fear of the unknown and providing confidence that its achievement is possible. Because the cost of change is always high in terms of uncertainty and upheaval, it is always important to accentuate the benefits of the overall goal and link it to the strategy. Looking at this as an equation, we can see that we are more likely to deliver change if the multiplying effect of A, B and D is higher than the cost of change.

A good strategy creates a vision that provides meaning for those within the organization and may trigger images and emotions that can bond people together in pursuit of a common purpose. We all like to have a sense of purpose and find greater importance in what we are doing, perhaps to feel part of something bigger than ourselves. There is a frequently recounted story about President John F. Kennedy that illustrates this concept. Apparently, while touring NASA, he stopped to speak to a janitor who was cleaning the floor. When asked about his job, rather than refer to the fact that he was mopping floors the janitor responded with pride: 'I'm helping to put a man on the moon'. Although this story may be apocryphal, it makes the point that we all want to feel part of something bigger than ourselves; if we want to influence people to behave in a certain way, we have to give them that sense of greater meaning. We can imagine that this is particularly important with changes that people really don't like, because providing that sense of meaning is much more powerful and sweetens the pill of having to change.

Unfortunately, during change we often focus on telling people 'what' to change rather than 'why', which often results in resistance. Metaphorically, it is like people are looking down at potential obstacles or problems without the motivation to overcome them. On the other hand, connecting with the strategy or vision encourages people to look up and to see the future first; it allows us to paint a picture of the future with or without the change. The future might be positive and exciting with the change, or it might be negative and frightening without the change. We discuss individual meta-programs in Chapter 4, which explains how some of us are motivated by positive or goal-oriented language and others are motivated away from perceived pain. Again, this concept reinforces the potential power of the Change Equation in delivering change effectively. The point is that people should feel able to understand the consequences of not changing by looking to the future.

To build and communicate these powerful links with a positive or negative association, we need to ensure that the 'why', 'what' and 'how' of any change are understood at all levels of the organization. There can be multiple 'whys', 'whats' and 'hows' to ensure relevance and meaning to different audiences.

Of course, strategies have to be based on assumptions about the future environment; therefore, the quality and credibility of the strategy will be directly related to the effectiveness of the assumptions. Tools like Porter and Tanner's (2003) PESTLE analysis can be used to ensure that the rationale for any strategy change is well evidenced.

Political factors

This may include likely government policies or changes, including tariffs, subsidies or immigration quotas, which can create perceived urgency, e.g., many businesses relying on consultants in full-time positions moved to outsource staff when National Insurance costs went up.

Economic factors

National and global economic circumstances, whether we are in a recession or boom times and exchange rates can all influence these factors, e.g., we may choose to extend our house rather than move in order to avoid Stamp Duty.

Social factors

This is more about the trends within society, including demographic and cultural changes in expectations for products, services and working environments, e.g., we may be influenced by what others who we consider to be of a similar demographic are doing, or we may be motivated to move jobs because we have friends in a particular industry.

Technological factors

Clearly, this is a rapidly changing and potentially disruptive force that can create competitive advantage in terms of goods, services and access to both customers and workforce, e.g., we may need to change processes to make goods available online or develop an online app for customer feedback.

Legal factors

New legislation can provide compelling reasons to change in relation to governance, e.g., the General Data Protection Regulation (GDPR), or legislation that provides new market opportunities for products or solutions.

Environmental factors

This relates to what is happening around us, including changing attitudes on environmental practices. This can be bolstered by government legislation (legal) or incentives, e.g., tax relief on green company cars (economic), which may make change more attractive.

Strategies may also be influenced by the level of competition in a specific marketplace; this could be about new products, companies driving prices down or the increasing bargaining power of buyers or suppliers. These potential opportunities or threats tend to bring additional urgency to any strategy, helping it to become more compelling and potentially easier for people to identify with.

As we have established, the purpose of a strategy is to enable organizations or businesses to survive and prosper, usually by meeting customer needs profitably or sustainably. If the ability to achieve this purpose is threatened, then it creates the need to change. This creates urgency and helps people to realize that things can't stay as they are. Consider the example of a company restructure that is going to involve redundancies or job losses. Very often this is a painful and unpopular form of change. However, if people understand the consequences of no job cuts – perhaps the business will be so unprofitable that it will no longer be viable and therefore will close – then they will understand that the change is necessary and will buy in to the rationale. They can then focus on how the change is delivered to ensure the best outcomes for those affected. The restructure doesn't have to be a negative vision; it could also offer a positive vision of a reskilled workforce that is able to beat the competition due to its enhanced skills and productivity.

This is all about how we re-frame or re-position a message before we communicate it. So, connecting with strategy is also about inspiring people to look to the future, helping them to consider the vision of change and to understand *why* in terms that are relevant to them. We have probably heard the term 'golden thread' being referred to when setting objectives. Essentially, if we understand the 'golden thread' – the link between our goals or objectives and the overall business strategy – then we understand why we are doing what we are doing, or, in this case, why the change is necessary. This is beneficial in several ways, first, it gives purpose and meaning, as outlined earlier, particularly if we can understand the direct link between our own activities or interests and the vision for change. Second, it empowers us to make our own decisions about how best to deliver the change. This is incredibly helpful when it comes to delivering large-scale change, which requires groups of people to take forward a future vision. Clarity about the overall purpose or strategy that we are trying to deliver acts like a compass, stabilizing us and ensuring that we stay on track.

Consider an example of a new company process that requires all contractors to complete detailed timesheets with a breakdown of how much time was spent with which customer. This will be time-consuming and therefore costly, either to the contractor or to the company. So, what is the purpose or strategy behind this new process? When we follow the golden thread through the organization, we find that the actual purpose is to better allocate training costs to clients, to ensure that all training is billed accurately. A blanket cascade of the new process without understanding would result in wasted time or money for half of contractors, many of whom work on pre-defined projects or temporarily fulfil internal roles. The golden thread also emphasizes that the most important piece of information to be captured by the contractors involved in customer training is which customers they are spending the most time on; it is not about micro-accounting for time.

All often, a blanket approach is taken when cascading new processes whereby people don't understand the overall strategy or purpose of the change. This can lead to two problems: an inappropriate and possibly damaging new process is implemented more widely than required, or people see that the process is inappropriate and don't follow through, which means the desired changes are not made. Understanding the overall 'why' as well as the 'what' or 'how' makes a huge difference when change is cascaded down an organization. Change Agents should have the courage to go back up the chain to question the purpose of a cascaded change, ensuring that it hasn't been lost during the roll-out.

Of course, strategies and visions tend to be long-term, so however inspiring they are to begin with, they still require high levels of determination and resilience to see them through to fruition. It is no wonder so many change efforts fail to reap all of the benefits that were originally envisioned. It is challenging to keep focused and to stay on track over the long term, which is why we should also set key sub-goals or milestones along the way. This allows us to focus ourselves and others on more manageable, short-term deliverables in the confidence that they are taking us in the right direction over the longer term. This golden thread of alignment supported by short-term goals helps people to choose the best activities or behaviours when faced with uncertainty, which is so often the case in times of change. In the absence of leadership or immediate direction, by understanding and following the golden thread we are better able to decide on the best course of action ourselves in order to deliver the goal or strategy in question.

As Change Agents, we and others need to be able to clearly articulate answers to the following questions.

- Where are we now?
- Where do we need to go?
- Why do we need to go there?
- How will we get there (specifically)?

Most people are familiar with the concept of SMART goals – specific and stretching, measurable, achievable and agreed, relevant and time-bound. However, SMART really is far more than an acronym; it is well backed by behavioural science. Research shows that goals that people consider to be stretching yet achievable are actually more motivational than extremely easy goals. One of the most effective ways of encouraging high performance is by agreeing clear goals and providing feedback against them (Locke & Latham, 1994). I use the term 'agreed' intentionally because it is the involvement of the individual in setting the goal that increases buy-in and presumably motivation. Involvement is key to buy-in when setting goals and delivering change.

'Relevant' means relevant to the business strategy, so it is all about the golden thread, as discussed earlier. It means ensuring the individual understands the relevance of the goal in relation to the strategy and potentially in relation to their own role or their own interests. The more relevant to us we consider a goal to be, the greater our buy-in and motivation to pursue it.

Finally, any goal needs to be time-bound, to allow us to choose when to review it. This is particularly important in large-scale change that can go on for months or even years. There should be an overall target date or timescale to aim for and if this is months or years out then it is advisable to define a series of milestones with timelines. This helps to provide a sense of progress, keeping people focused and on track. Without milestones, it is easy for people to lose focus and for any progress to stop or even be reversed. As Change Agents, we need to help people to connect with the vision or strategy and to agree and define project plans with milestones that will take us from where we are now to where we want to be.

When we set strategies and goals it is easy for us to focus purely on hard, tangible metrics, yet we know that failure to address cultural or people issues is often at the root of many change failures. Nohria and Beer (2000) describe two basic theories of change that should be balanced in order to deliver sustainable change. The first, Theory E change, emphasizes hard economic value such as shareholder return, in effect being about cost savings or increased profitability through redundancies or the sale of a business. The second, Theory O change, is about developing corporate culture and human capability, effectively building intrinsic value into a company that will be realized later, through the skills, knowledge and motivation of the staff. In reality, most companies attempt to balance both theories during change. However, this approach needs to be carefully managed to prevent leadership from looking erratic by erring between savage cost-cutting and cultural development. As always, connecting with strategy is relevant here as there may be a harder, financial goal supported by a softer, cultural vision. Usually, the cultural vision is more motivational for people to buy in to but more challenging to be specific about when setting goals. It is worth persisting here and sometimes identifying success indicators can be helpful if the goal feels a little intangible. For example, we may want to increase our share price through increased sales and customer retention as our Theory E measure. In order to increase the sales and retain customers we may need to increase our customer satisfaction by developing the skills and behaviours of our workforce, which is a measure more associated with Theory O. Success measures may be levels of customer retention, net promoter scores and salesperson knowledge levels across our product range. Both are tangible and they align and support the overall strategy.

Of course, we can communicate a vision and strategy and set SMART goals, but there will still be obstacles and resistance to overcome. Chan Kim and Mauborgne's (2003) *Harvard Business Review* article 'Tipping Point Leadership' can be useful when bringing strategy to life. Their four-step approach can be used to overcome some of the many hurdles.

Break through the cognitive hurdle.

> Consider how you can help your audience to experience the problem rather than consider it as abstract. Storytelling is a helpful technique to use here; gather real examples of the problems or customer needs that are creating the need to change. Maybe the audience would benefit from hearing directly from customers (if not in person, via salespeople or video) how your business or product is perceived? Consider how you can bring the problem to life.

Sidestep the resource hurdle.

> Another way of explaining this might be with the term 'choose your battles'. This is about focusing

resources on the areas of change that will make the biggest difference first. Don't try to achieve everything at once; identify some quick wins and deliver them. If we are setting goals and milestones, as suggested, then make the earliest milestones the ones that will make the biggest difference and don't try to achieve too many things at once.

Jump the motivational hurdle.

Rather than trying to change the organization en-masse, identify key influencers within the business who can do this for you. Consider the ripple effect if you drop a stone into a pool of water. By identifying the right influencers and getting them on board, potentially as fellow Change Agents, we can leverage their networks to deliver change rapidly.

Knock over the political hurdle.

Even when change is about to take place and the tipping point is reached there will still be resistors and possibly even saboteurs who want to cling onto the old way. Remember the story from Chapter 1 about the cynical operations director who had the potential to undermine the whole change initiative? Identify these people up front, particularly if they are senior, and have the courage to involve them and get them on board. If they feel like the change is their idea, we are far more likely to succeed.

Connecting with strategy is about creating the 'why' for change; it creates people with the vision and motivation to want to change. It also sets key milestones and goals that keep the change on track. The Change Superpowers that are most helpful are a diverse mix of painting visual pictures, storytelling, goal-setting and even project management.

Case study in brief: modernizing a membership organization

Company info: scientific membership organization; 500 people.

Background: although financially lucrative and publishing a number of highly respected scientific journals monthly, the organization was considered old-fashioned and was turning away 80% of the content sent for publication as the research was not considered ground-breaking enough. A new CEO came in and felt that this was a wasteful and short-sighted strategy.

Action: he tried to convince the organization of the need to change by sharing a commercial vision around increased profitability and a wider audience if it increased the number of publications and used more of the content. However, this strategy didn't resonate with the audience and was resisted. Through consultation with stakeholders, the CEO realized that a better strategy and message was about how increased profit could be used: for greater investment into research. He also defined the purpose and audience for each journal, showing how it would further research opportunities.

Result: the organization bought into this strategy and went through a major restructure and realignment. Within two years it was publishing double the number of journals monthly, with significantly increased readership and profitability, and was recognized for its contribution back into the scientific community.

Quick recap on connecting with strategy

- Connecting with strategy is about providing people with a vision and reason to change.
- The vision for change should provide purpose and be meaningful at all levels of the organization.
- Communicate the 'why', 'what' and 'how' of change up and down the organization.
- Use stories and emotions to create urgency and help people understand the consequences of not changing.
- The future strategy should be broken into smaller SMART milestones to keep on track.

Online toolkit

The following free change resources can be downloaded via: www.changesuperhero.com
- The 'Five Superpowers of a Change Superhero' quiz
- The 'Five Superpowers of a Change Superhero' infographic

CHAPTER 3

Corroboration

No one wants advice, just corroboration.
John Steinbeck

Change is so much easier when people don't feel coerced or pressured into having to change against their will. In the last chapter we discussed the value of motivators in providing a vision and sense of meaning to gain buy-in. This chapter will highlight the third Change Superpower: the ability to provide corroboration or evidence for the need to change. Most people are quite invested in retaining the status quo and won't simply change without perceived evidence of the need to do so. As John Steinbeck says, we don't want advice, just corroboration. We don't want subjective opinions or advice; we need evidence for the need to change in the form of facts, figures or real-life examples that seem relevant to our situation.

We need evidence or persuasion that this change is in our best interests and different from those that have taken place and failed before. We need to be given rational and emotional reasons to say 'yes' to the change. Change Superheroes understand the science of influencing others and use these persuasive skills to provide the rationale for change. It is important to understand that this is all about ethical influence, not manipulation or lies, and the true Change Superhero is able to distinguish between the two with integrity.

Shortcuts to influence

Robert Cialdini is well known for his research into the subject of influence and persuasion, as published in his book *Influence: The Psychology of Persuasion* (Cialdini, 2006). He outlines six shortcuts that we use as the basis for making decisions. When we understand how to communicate with these shortcuts, it is far easier to persuade others to say 'yes' to change, ethically.

The six shortcuts are authority, consensus, consistency, liking, reciprocity and scarcity. Some of these are obviously about using facts and figures to provide evidence. However, Cialdini's research also tells us that although we may consider ourselves to be influenced by logical facts and figures, some of our 'evidence' is far more subjective, or perhaps even emotional, although just as likely to be persuasive.

Let's look at each one in turn and consider how we can use our understanding of these shortcuts to persuade people of the benefits of any change that we are involved in delivering.

Authority

Authority is a great place to start because this can be an important influencer in relation to organizational change. In this context we are referring to validation of a course of action by a relevant and highly regarded or powerful authority. This could be an authoritative figure within the organization, such as the CEO or a board member who might be sponsoring the change. Alternatively, it could refer to external authorities, perhaps industry experts, governments or regulatory bodies. This form of influence relies on our desire to follow the lead of legitimate experts. This is a powerful driver, possibly because we learn from an early age to trust people in uniform or respect our elders.

In the context of change, it is particularly important to ensure that the authority we are referring to is relevant to the audience concerned. So, if we are looking to provide evidence for change to a UK financial services audience, we might refer to the relevant professional body, such as the Financial Conduct Authority (FCA). If we are aiming to influence a medical audience, we may allude to evidence in the *Lancet*. The more legitimate the authority in the eyes of our audience, the greater the chance that it will influence them to want to change.

One final use of authority that we have probably all experienced is that of legal requirements. Many changes have been driven through effectively because they were underpinned by legal or regulatory requirements. We would label this kind of change compliance, and it is pretty powerful – I need only mention the term GDPR for many European readers to appreciate this. Influential though compliance is, it is not the same as buy-in; it is more a case of reluctant commitment. So, when we are managing change where the authority being referenced is legal or regulatory, it is worth thinking about balancing out this influence with other more positive motivators, like those below, to encourage greater buy-in.

Consensus or social proof

Our need for consensus probably stems from our innate human instinct to be part of a group. This is related to a concept called social proof, where we seek assurance that others have also bought into an idea before making the decision to buy in ourselves. As with authority, we seek social proof from people or businesses like us. So, if we wanted to influence using social proof, we would use examples of other organizations in a similar industry or a similar customer who applied this change strategy successfully.

Many of us don't realize how often we are influenced by or rely on social proof. Remember the story of 'the First Follower' in our chapter on courage? The first, second and subsequent followers provided the social evidence that it was safe to dance like the crazy person. Once a critical mass of followers was reached, there was greater pressure to be part of the crowd than to remain a bystander, and people started to join in hordes. This is a key principle to remember as a Change Agent: it is hard to gain the first few followers as the social proof is weaker, but the more we can build, the easier it is to tip the majority. Just consider the power of TripAdvisor, Glassdoor or Amazon reviews to appreciate the power of social proof. Most of us will rely on reviews when shopping online, or personal recommendations when seeking out a new handyman. The more we identify with the person providing the reference or recommendation, the more likely we are to be influenced by it. Social proof was used to great effect (even if somewhat tongue-in-cheek) in adverts by a cat-food manufacturer for many years. Many readers will remember the strapline 'nine out of ten cats prefer Cat Food X' to this day and may consider it a premium brand due to that powerful campaign. In business we can emulate this by providing case studies or references that provide evidence that other customers (like us) bought and liked the product.

So, bringing this back to corroborating the need for change, we need to have examples of how this change was necessary or worked in other, similar environments. It may be that the biggest competitor in the same industry has just made the same change and it has saved them a certain amount of money or increased their competitiveness. Alternatively, we may share how someone in a similar role or department made this same career change or decision and it worked out well for them. Using consensus or social proof to influence is subjective but effective. It makes people feel reassured that others like them are making the same decision. We are drawn to feeling part of the group and prefer not to go against it.

Consistency

This is our third influencing short-cut, which Cialdini describes as being like personal congruence. Essentially, we want to be seen as being consistent; if we say 'yes' to something, however small, we are more likely to then say 'yes' to something similar but bigger in future. We experience this with donations to charity, for example. We might sign up to donate £3.00 per month then, after a while, be contacted to donate a little bit more and so on. It is significantly easier for a charity to get an existing supporter to increase their current donation than it is to gain a new donor. Small, incremental changes are less noticeable, and this principle of consistency means they can soon build up to be quite significant.

So, if we take a business example – say, we want to make potential changes to working hours – we might ask people to make a small adjustment in hours initially and then increase this over time. The problem here is that people can resent this approach if they feel manipulated. With the charity example, we feel pressure to say 'yes' to an increase in the donation because we are already supporters, yet we may also resent feeling trapped into paying more. My sense is that Change Superheroes use consistency with caution to influence people.

Good ways of using consistency, as a way of influencing for change, are when dealing with concerns. Very often when presented with change, people tend to focus on what is changing rather than what is staying the same. For example, a restructure that can feel like a huge change to people will still have plenty of consistency if we look for it. We may have a change in manager, but we are still doing the same job, with the same colleagues, in the same office with the same hours and the same commute. Often, when we help people to view change like this, they realize that there is still plenty of consistency. In fact, this whole concept is supported by findings in neuroscience that show that the fight-or-flight response in our brains is triggered by the extent to which we perceive certainty and fairness. If people can feel a level of certainty and fairness in a change then it is less likely to invoke their flight response. Of course, the opposite is also true – if we feel that the change is being handled unfairly or has inconsistencies within it then we are more likely to react against it or run away from it.

Liking

Fundamentally this is about rapport; we tend to like people that we consider to be similar to us in terms of values, views, circumstances, upbringing or even supporting the same football team. If we feel we have something in common with someone then we trust them, and we are more likely to be convinced by people we like and trust. There are similarities to social proof here, but I would say that the social proof of liking someone is more unconscious. That means we decide whether we like people through things like body language, eye contact and whether we believe they are interested in and like *us*. Some people are naturally good at these unconscious skills of being likeable and others are less so, but they can be learned. If we are planning to be a Change Superhero, then building self-awareness about our unconscious 'likeability' signals is a great idea. A few ways in which we can build this understanding follow.

Ask for feedback from friends or colleagues about how your body language and levels of eye contact come across. Do they feel that your body language comes over as consistently friendly or do you sometimes come across as a little defensive or closed? It is particularly helpful if you can get feedback from someone who has seen you communicate with someone new or in an awkward situation. We are aiming to come over as open and warm, so smiling and eye contact go a long way.

Consider how good you are at taking a genuine interest in other people. Do you ask them open questions about themselves such as where they have worked or what job they do? Do you listen carefully to the responses and build on them? Or do you tend to jump around, change the subject or perhaps not ask many questions at all? It is worth being aware of our natural tendency to ask questions about people because it makes us seem interested. Additionally, when we find out small nuggets of information, we are better able to demonstrate commonality with similarities of our own that build rapport. For instance, if I asked someone where they had worked and they named a big player in a certain industry, I may be able to build rapport by sharing that I, too, had worked in the same industry. The conversation may even progress to when we worked there and whether we knew similar people. Another example is picking up on accents and finding out that you may share similar geographic roots. This happens naturally in every conversation when we are getting to know people and finding common ground is a key skill when building rapport and trust.

If we don't have time to get to know people as individuals, a quick way of building rapport is by finding something to compliment about someone. This is something anyone can learn to do – but it must be sincere and not too personal in the workplace. So, we might compliment someone on a tie, watch or scarf but I would advise steering clear of physical attributes. Even better is a specific compliment about something that they have said or done, such as: 'I really liked the way you handled that difficult question that James asked' or 'The way you explained that research study was really clear and helpful – thank you'. This is simply the skill of good workplace feedback and we would all benefit from developing this.

In circumstances where we are communicating one to many, we can use humour or self-deprecation to build rapport with a larger audience. When we laugh together, we share the same experience and feel that we like the person who made us laugh. If humour is inappropriate due to the nature of the change, then sincerely sharing our own feelings without being over-emotional is one of the best things we can do to demonstrate our likeability and convince others that our message is valid.

Exchange

Our fifth influencing strategy is the concept of reciprocity or exchange. Exchange is linked to the well-known reciprocation principle, where if you give someone something, even of low value, they naturally feel indebted and a pressure to reciprocate or give something back. Cialdini explains how tips went up by 3% in restaurants where a waiter provided a mint or a liquor at the end of a meal. This experiment went on to show that when the number of the mints doubled, tips didn't double – they quadrupled! However, perhaps most interesting was the fact that if the waiter walked away from the table and then came back with a personalized comment such as 'For you nice people, I am going to give you an extra mint', tips went through the roof. This shows how powerful the instinct to reciprocate is and the scale of this can be increased by personalizing the initial gift.

The key with reciprocation is that the power sits with the person who gives something first. This knowledge can be used when negotiating, by using concessions. This principle suggests that offering a concession will increase the chances of the other side also making a concession.

In the context of change, we can use this knowledge to consider how we can provide potential reciprocation in the form of concessions that may 'sweeten the pill' of change. Examples could be enhancements to a redundancy package, such as garden leave or retraining and support in finding a new job. Of course, these will only be considered part of a fair exchange if the individual concerned feels that they are over and above the norm. The challenge is predicting people's actual expectations in order to understand whether the exchange will be deemed positive and therefore increase buy-in.

Scarcity

Finally, scarcity is also an effective influencing tool, although it should be used with caution as it can feel manipulative. It is a frequently used marketing ploy; we might be told to buy now, before the product or service runs out. However, we can legitimately use this knowledge when communicating change to create urgency. For example, 'if we don't change our business strategy now, we are likely to miss out on specific market opportunities'. It could also be used in relation to redundancy, where we may be able to offer a small number of voluntary redundancies within a certain time frame. Again, this should be used with caution because any organizational change must be considered fair and equal and offering specialist terms for some based on how quickly they commit to the changing circumstances could be contrary to employment law.

Next time you come across communication about the need to change, consider how many of these influencing styles have been included. Sadly, most corporate change messaging lacks influence and comes across as generic and bland. Remember, the power of using legitimate influence is that it persuades us that the change is in our interest or necessary. This helps people to come to terms with the reason for the change, accept it and get on board. Some of us may find some influencing styles more convincing than others. However, most of us will accept the need for change more readily if we experience a range of persuasive reasons to buy in. Persuading people to change is a more positive experience for everybody and the change is more likely to stick because people choose to change rather than feeling coerced.

Case study in brief: reducing resistance through influence and corroboration

Company info: charity; 150 people.

Background: a publishing charity was considered by many to be performing steadily within its sector. A new CEO took over and saw that it would be under serious threat within five years unless it increased productivity and modernized the way it worked through restructuring (working across the organization rather than in long-standing silos). The existing workforce considered themselves to be high performers and had little or no appetite for change. People had a vested interest in things remaining the same and financially the business was still profitable so the employees didn't understand the need for change.

Action: the CEO brought in an HR Change Agent who helped to design structural changes as well as managing a series of communications explaining the business rationale for the change (logical reasoning) with evidence for the need to change and support mechanisms in place for those affected (exchange). There was significant cultural resistance and this was addressed through empathizing and listening to concerns and coaching managers (rapport) and the senior management team to stay on message supporting the change (consistency) with face-to-face communication and the publication of a series of FAQs.

Result: within a few weeks people started to accept the change and speak about it positively and optimistically. They started planning how to make it work practically, arranging to transfer knowledge proactively. Commitment, morale and alignment with the 2030 vision is now high.

Quick recap on corroboration

- We can influence others to change by providing relevant evidence that change is necessary or desirable.
- It is more effective to persuade people to want to change than to coerce them.
- When using influencing styles, they must be sincere to avoid appearing manipulative.
- Understanding the science of influence is key to persuasion.
- When planning to communicate change, incorporate as many different types of influence as possible.

Online toolkit

The following free change resources can be downloaded via: www.changesuperhero.com

- Influencing styles infographic
- The 'Five Superpowers of a Change Superhero' quiz
- The 'Five Superpowers of a Change Superhero' infographic

CHAPTER 4

Communication

You *cannot* **not** *communicate.*
Paul Watzlawick

N ow that we have brought people with us in recognizing and engaging in the need for change we will need to start to embark on a communications journey. This chapter will look at why we need to communicate, as well as examining the different forms of communication that we, as successful Change Superheroes, will need to understand and use as appropriate. Aspects of neuro-linguistic programming (NLP), such as learned filters and meta-programs, will all be explored in this chapter.

That we have no choice but to communicate is the message behind this chapter's epigraph and is a hugely important lesson for us to take on board. Communication is our fourth Change Superpower and is of course far more than simply telling people to change. We need to be aware that we are continually communicating through everything we say or do. It is vital that we learn to listen more than we speak and ensure that our non-verbal communication is aligned with our verbal messaging if we want others to trust us.

Our ability to communicate effectively with a wide range of people is almost certainly the most important skill that we have when it comes to delivering change. John Kotter is a Harvard professor and renowned expert on large-scale business change. We explain his eight-step model for change (Kotter, 1995) in detail in Chapter 13, and communication is a common theme throughout. It is Kotter's view that we rarely communicate frequently or effectively enough about business change. In fact, he estimates that we should communicate ten times more than we think we should for the message to be fully understood and acted on. Personally, I would add the importance of considering *how* we communicate, just as much as the frequency.

Most organizations could improve both the frequency and the quality of their change communication, so we will consider communication from both an individual and organizational level within this book. Chapters 11 and 12 give step-by-step examples of how to plan and communicate large-scale change. However, we need to start by communicating with the individual and that is the focus of this chapter. We start by considering the different ways in which we communicate consciously and unconsciously and move on to explore aspects of NLP that can give clues to our subconscious motivations. Understanding this can be hugely valuable to us as Change Agents. Finally, we consider the important but often overlooked skill of listening and explain the value of subtle differences in style.

More than what we say: understanding how we communicate

We are always communicating, even when we are not speaking, so our subconscious thoughts or emotions may be portrayed regardless of whether or not that is our intent. When delivering messages around change we need to understand the many, different ways in which we are communicating, so that the message we portray is the one that we want others to receive.

In the 1960s, Albert Meharabian (1981) carried out research into how we communicate feelings and attitudes when speaking to others. His original work has often been misquoted, which has led to some misunderstanding, so needs to be used in context. He identified, perhaps surprisingly at the time, that the words we use represent a very small proportion of the meaning *that is taken* from communication. Far more is understood by others through our tone of voice and facial expressions. His findings were that the proportions of meaning we take from different sources during a conversation are as follows:

- words used (7%)

- tone of voice (38%)
- facial expressions and body language (55%)

The key here is that we seem to give away our conscious or unconscious feelings and attitudes in these ways when communicating. When we are preparing to communicate change, we are very likely to prepare our message carefully in the form of words. However, Meharabian's work suggests how important it is for us to rehearse the *way* we deliver a message in terms of tonality and body language, particularly if we have strong personal feelings about the change. This can work to our advantage if we feel positive about the change, as our unspoken feelings are likely to reinforce our words. However, if we are less comfortable about the message then our tone of voice and body language could well give this away. Most of us have seen *James Bond* films where a card player's 'tell' is identified, giving away the fact that he is bluffing about his hand. In the same way, we all have our own unconscious idiosyncrasies that are communicating alongside our words and it is helpful for us to be aware of their potential impact.

The term 'body language' is a familiar one, but it is probably helpful to spell out some examples of what we really mean by this. Facial expressions and body language include behaviours like posture – are our arms or legs crossed or open? Do we use particular hand gestures or tilt our head in a certain way? In terms of facial expressions, are our brows raised or lowered? Do we furrow our brows, hold eye contact or look away?

We communicate emotions through our vocal intonation, through our levels of inflection, pitch and pace. For example, we may speak more quickly when we are excited or nervous. Having a lower-pitched voice is commonly interpreted as being more authoritative. Margaret Thatcher apparently received a lot of voice coaching to lower the pitch of her voice in order to sound more authoritative in her role as the first female prime minister of the UK.

Neuro-linguistic programming

Sensory preferences

Obviously, the words we choose should be most relevant to our message. However, those who study a branch of psychology known as neuro-linguistic programming (NLP) believe that many of us prefer a certain category of sensory-based language that is likely to be predominantly visual, auditory or kinaesthetic (feeling). So, if we prefer visual terminology, we may be more likely to use words and phrases such as 'see', 'look', 'view', 'foggy', 'clear', 'bright', 'reveal', 'focused', 'picture this' etc.

If we have a preference for auditory language then we may include language like 'sound', 'hear', 'tell', 'listen', 'resonate', 'loud-and-clear', 'tune in/out', 'on another note', 'give me your ear' etc., and if we have a preference for kinaesthetic or feeling language we might use terms like 'touch', 'feel', 'grasp', 'fuzzy', 'hard', 'concrete', 'solid', 'unfeeling', 'heated debate', 'make contact' etc.

Now, personally I believe that most of us use a range of sensory terms and they may be a better indicator of our environment than our sensory preferences. However, I have witnessed people using different sensory terminology with each other and seeming to struggle to communicate. An example would be someone saying: 'I just can't picture it', with the colleague responding, 'Let me talk you through it again'. This is a visual/auditory mismatch, whereas the response 'Let me show you want I mean' would be a visual/visual match.

Rapport

To understand what I mean by matching or mismatching, we first need to understand the concept of rapport, defined as a shared understanding or state of mutual trust. Behavioural research shows that mirroring and matching – unconsciously copying other people's body language and mannerisms and repeating their words – helps build trust and establishes rapport. When we feel naturally comfortable with others, we do this instinctively, but it is also a skill we can learn and develop.

As we might imagine, mirroring is when we literally copy or reflect the gestures or facial expressions of another person, as if looking in a mirror. When people demonstrate this naturally, there is a genuine sense of being understood, as if the other person is reflecting our emotions back to us.

Matching, on the other hand, usually has a built-in 'time lag'. For example, if the person we are communicating with uncrosses their legs and leans slightly inward while speaking, we might wait for a few seconds and then discretely adopt the same posture. Matching is more subtle than mirroring; we may cross our arms or ankles to match someone's crossed legs. It doesn't have to be a mirror-match. We talked earlier about people having preferences for different sensory terminology and we can choose to match in this way as well. Someone may say, 'I am still just feeling my way through this', to which you might reply, 'I am happy to walk it through again, if that would help'. This would be a kinaesthetic match and could be another way of 'speaking the same language' and building rapport.

There are a couple of health warnings here; the first is that mirroring should be done discretely and naturally to appear authentic, otherwise it will appear to be mimicking and is more likely to break rapport. The second point is that it is only helpful to mirror or match others when the emotions are constructive to reflect. If we are listening to someone in a rage, we don't want to portray anger back at them because their anger may escalate. We may want to mismatch (which will break rapport) or try something more subtle: pacing and leading. This is where we may gain or maintain rapport by reflecting the tempo of the communication, nodding our head slightly in time with the pace of the language and then gradually slowing down the nodding, perhaps leading the other person to calm down.

As we might imagine, behaviours that mismatch are more likely to damage rapport and break trust between individuals. So, we need to be aware of how congruent or aligned our words, tone of voice and body language are when we are delivering messages around change. I have found that one of the best ways of doing this is by ensuring that our thoughts about our message are positive and we are clear about what and why we are delivering it. If we do that, it is highly likely that our body language will also be positive. Start with your mindset and your body will follow.

Meta-programs

Staying with the topic of NLP, let us move into a deeper understanding of the way in which the words or language we choose gives insight into how our brain works. Rodger Bailey created a model called the Language and Behaviour (LAB) Profile that went on to become well known in the 1980s and 1990s identifying a set of patterns, called meta-programs, that are based on our own experiences, background and disposition. His LAB Profile was designed to adapt these meta-programs for use in the workplace. We use these filters to interpret the world and we give clues to these through our linguistic patterns – the way we talk – hence the term neuro-linguistic.

These meta-programs are context-specific; they are not the same as personality preferences but they can give clues to the ways in which we are motivated. When we understand how someone is motivated, we can tailor our language to make it more influential to people. There are many categories of meta-program, but I am going to focus on the following three because I believe them to be most relevant to us as Change Agents.

Towards versus away motivation

This could also be referred to as 'carrot-and-stick' motivation as it is where a person is motivated towards a goal or away from pain. Shelle Rose Charvet, in her book

Words that Change Minds (1997), describes her research on meta-programs. She suggests that about 20% of us are mainly towards-motivated; 20% are away-motivated and the rest are a combination of both. What does this mean to us as Change Agents? Well, when we are thinking about motivating others to change we need have both 'towards' and 'away' language in our communications kitbag to ensure that the change message appeals to everyone. For instance, 'towards' language may be about painting the picture of an exciting new future, whereas an 'away' message would be more about avoiding the pain of an undesirable current or future situation.

Best-case versus worst-case-scenario thinking

It seems that this meta-program was identified by Michael Hall and Bob Bodenhamer in their book *Figuring Out People* (2006) and is similar to the concept of 'towards' and 'away' motivation. They describe it as follows. Best-case versus worst-case-scenario thinking could be akin to optimism or pessimism, or the concept of seeing the glass half-full or half-empty. It is about what we first focus on – positive opportunities and possibilities, or risks and potential threats.

Highly relevant to change, this meta-program is distinguished by its specific reference to the future, the formation of expectations, predictability, control and beliefs about possibilities. Clearly, working with people who look for positive possibilities is easier in terms of initial buy-in than those who look for the worst case when rolling out change. However, if we think about building our Change Team, it can be extremely helpful to have someone who considers the worst-case scenario in order to spot potential risks up front and plan for them. Similarly, having a Change Team full of optimistic best-case thinkers can be unrealistic and set us up for failure. When managing change, it is definitely a good idea to create a vision of the best case but with a plan to mitigate the worst.

Similarities versus differences

As the name would suggest, some people are attuned to looking for similarities, whereas others focus on differences. In times of change it can be the case that people focus all their attention on what is going to actually change even though the majority of the circumstances are going to remain the same. As Change Agents, we can reassure people by highlighting all the things that are staying the same within a situation to keep the areas of change or difference proportionate. For example, we may be moving offices, which involves a different commute to work and different desk etc. However, we will still have the same working hours, manager and team.

Learned filters

In addition to these meta-programs, NLP also teaches us that there are three learned filters, or shortcuts, through which we view the world: deletion, distortion and generalization.

As with many thought processes and beliefs, we usually learned them before the age of 7 years old, when our highly impressionable subconscious mind was like a sponge, taking on experiences and creating rules from them. Essentially, these are shortcuts that serve us well in much of life but can need managing carefully when they are used to respond to change.

Deletion

This is when we unconsciously ignore certain pieces of information in order to reinforce our existing view of the world. In a change situation, this may mean we don't 'hear' certain pieces of information. Perhaps if we have a belief that the company doesn't care about people, we won't 'hear' the messages where the company is trying to do its best for them. We can help by gently pointing out where pieces of information have been overlooked or deleted, e.g., 'I believe that the benefits package being offered is better than any other in the market'.

Distortion

This is when we take reality and twist it. This can be helpful when we are trying to be humorous or creative, but can also be difficult when we may extrapolate meaning that wasn't intended from a situation or someone's behaviour. For example, we may hear someone who has been objectively placed into a group 'at risk' of redundancy state, 'I knew that they didn't like me'. This could put the perceived fairness of the process in danger with others. If we are dealing with distortion, then we need to keep returning to the facts, ideally with evidence, e.g., 'I know HR had the redundancy criteria and assessments checked for objectivity, so I am sure nothing is personal'.

Generalization

This is when we take a few examples of a behaviour and create a general principle. It is a bit like distortion, but the application is broader – 'This sort of thing always happens' or 'Everyone else is getting special treatment'. The best way to deal with other people's generalizations is to ask for specifics, e.g., 'Who has had special treatment?' or 'What specifically has happened in the past that is the same?' Usually, it becomes clear that there are really just a couple of examples, and this allows us to put the generalization into context.

Empathic listening

Finally, one of the most important points to make about communication is that it isn't just about what we say. It is also about how we listen and what we hear. Communication is a two-way process and in each of the examples above we wouldn't respond appropriately if we hadn't listened fully to the communication from others. Listening appropriately means taking the words on board, listening to the tone of voice and observing the body language that others use to recognize the attitudes or emotions behind the communication. As Change Agents, it is our job to show that we have *really* heard the message that others are portraying, even if it is sometimes non-verbal. Listening is a skill unto itself and is a vital part of being an effective communicator.

Many of us have heard of the term 'active listening', which is when we listen hard to what the other person is saying, nod our head, make eye contact and demonstrate positive body language. When they pause for breath, we may actively respond to their point or put our own view forward. Active listening is a highly appropriate skill for many aspects of change – as long as we are fully listening and not just waiting for the other person to draw breath so that we can make our own point. However, change is often emotive and active listening may come over as confrontational in certain circumstances. This is when empathic listening is most helpful as a skill we should develop and use.

I first came across the concept of empathic listening in Stephen Covey's best-selling business book *The 7 Habits of Highly Effective People* (1989). Having been a trainer of this material, I was lucky enough to become really familiar with it, and I highly recommend it. Covey defines empathic listening as the highest form of listening. He explains that the purpose is *not* listening until we understand, but listening until the other person feels understood. He considered it like 'emotional oxygen', giving people the chance to breathe and relax. Clearly, during difficult times this is a powerful skill in helping others to process change. Later, when we discuss the natural emotional reactions that people go through during change, we will fully appreciate how useful this skill is in certain circumstances.

So, how do we learn to demonstrate empathic listening? Fundamentally, we are listening for the emotion below the spoken words. It really isn't about responding, other than to use non-words like 'Mmmhmm' or 'Go on, tell me more'. Obviously, our body language and facial expressions demonstrate our wish to understand. The idea is to allow the other person to truly express how they feel because then we will understand the true root of the problem. So, unlike active listening, we should restrain ourselves from asking probing questions until the emotion has subsided. Instead, it is better to reflect empathically the emotions that you believe the person is demonstrating, e.g., 'That sounds frustrating?' or 'That must feel exhausting?'. Notice the question mark at the end of each statement; this is important because we are guessing the person's emotion – we cannot be sure. However, we can feel pleased with our skills when we get an emphatic response of 'Yes, very!' (or sometimes less so when we hear 'No, it was more irritating than frustrating'). Either way, we are demonstrating a humble intent to truly understand and empathize with the other person's emotions. Empathic listening doesn't need to be used for long periods of time – just when the emotions are strong. After that we can move to more active listening and problem-solving. Empathic listening is a key ingredient within our toolkit and is useful in building strong relationships in all aspects of our lives, including during change.

So, this chapter has been about understanding the sheer breadth and depth of communication. It is a skill that we should learn and practise as there is so much more to it than just the words we say. The frequency and style with which we communicate during a change programme will make a significant difference to the overall success of the programme. Not only that, being a great communicator is probably one of the most useful life skills that we can all develop.

Case study in brief: using NLP to deal with the actively disengaged

Company info: manufacturing; 250 people.

Background: a company was delivering a culture change initiative and decided to carry out a 'human audit' to understand the levels of engagement amongst staff. It determined that almost 10% of staff fell into the actively disengaged category, which was undermining the new culture.

Action: an HR consultant coached managers on more proactive people management with every employee discussed at a monthly case management review. Managers became competent over time working on people risks consistently, using NLP techniques to understand where individuals were at and what it would take to have them personally engage, using NLP questioning and techniques to pace and lead individuals into a more empowered mindset.

Result: those who chose to leave went for the right reasons, empowered to move on, parting as friends in most cases. The company also witnessed a 70% increase in measurable employee engagement.

Quick recap on communication

- Our body language and intonation convey our attitudes and feelings more than our spoken or written words.
- During change it is hard to overcommunicate.
- People have different preferences in terms of how they absorb information.
- Matching or mismatching certain preferences can bring people along with us more effectively.
- Empathic listening is a powerful way of making people feel truly understood.

Online toolkit

The following free change resources can be downloaded via: www.changesuperhero.com

- NLP infographic
- The 'Five Superpowers of a Change Superhero' quiz
- The 'Five Superpowers of a Change Superhero' infographic

CHAPTER 5

Collaboration

*Alone we can do so little; together
we can do so much.*
Helen Keller

I t is not enough that we communicate with the people
involved in change; we have to do more, and the more we
can do is collaborate. This chapter will look at the different
skills needed for effective collaboration and highlight how
good collaboration is a natural extension of the platform
built by effective and engaging communication outlined in
the previous chapter.

We cannot deliver organizational change on our own. That is a fact. Yet, as Helen Keller says, 'together we can do so much'. We just need to learn to collaborate. During large-scale change, there are so many competing factors to consider, different viewpoints and challenges to overcome. Fundamentally, change will occur most effectively when everyone works together to go in the same direction.

So, what do we mean by the term collaboration? Simply put, it is two or more people working together to achieve a common goal, like cooperation or teamwork. However, we could also consider collaboration to be a mindset or attitude where we are looking to build something bigger and better by working with others. This is more than simply cooperating with others, which can sound quite passive or even reluctant. Collaboration as a Superpower is about always looking for ways in which people can benefit by working together across roles and silos. If we want to develop our collaborative mindset, we need to look for opportunities to achieve synergies when working with others. It is about thinking beyond our own needs to consider the needs of others and being creative in finding solutions to problems that work for everyone. In doing this we build stronger relationships, a sense of shared purpose and goodwill. This is an engine that can be extremely effective in delivering change. Although collaboration is about many people working together, it starts with an individual being collaborative, which in turn engages the First Follower outlined in Chapter 1. This chapter outlines the five key skills that we need to master in order to be collaborative and create our own movement.

The importance of collaboration is supported by the change studies of Rosabeth Kanter (2002), who found that change leaders who built coalitions were much more successful in delivering change. Kanter uses the term 'guiding coalition' in the same way as Kotter in his eight-step process for delivering change, covered in Chapter 13 (Kotter, 1995).

How to define collaboration

What do we mean by this term? My definition, for this purpose, is a tribe of like-minded individuals with complementary skills, all of whom are committed to do what it takes to deliver the change – our very own League of Change Superheroes with their own talents and strengths but sharing the same end goal. What I love about this analogy is the fact that Kanter actually uses the term 'Make everyone a hero' within her research. Everyone involved in delivering change is a Change Superhero, and this tribe expands as more and more people take on the challenge.

We've defined collaboration, but what does it look like? I would say that it is a natural extension of great communication and social skills along with an open and honest mindset. People who are collaborative demonstrate open, positive body language. They have the emotional intelligence to read the reactions of those around them when they are responding to a certain idea or situation and involve them when gathering feedback. This may be by asking open questions like 'What do you think about that idea?' or 'What would you suggest?', or it may involve a gentle challenge, e.g., 'You don't look so keen on that idea?'

The naturally collaborative Change Agent builds trust because they are clearly focused on achieving the most positive possible outcome for all concerned. They are unselfishly looking for a win/win solution to any problem and are *genuinely* interested in the wants and needs of others. Being collaborative is an active two-way process of gathering the thoughts, feedback and views of others while reflecting on open-ended questions about the wants, needs and potentially positive ways forward, for example, 'What could we do that would make this change better for your team?' or 'How could we move this situation forward positively?' Collaborative Change Agents are relentlessly and positively nudging the situation forwards at all times.

Campbell Macpherson (2017) uses the term 'Change Catalyst' in his book of the same name, and this epitomizes the type of collaboration that we are discussing here. A Change Catalyst fizzes and accelerates positive change reactions in others. They create synergies and outcomes that are potentially bigger than the sum of their parts. This is exactly what we are looking to achieve through collaboration.

Whether we are calling ourselves a Change Catalyst, Change Agent or Change Superhero, the purpose and importance of the role is the same. This role is all about collaboration; it is about working with others and harnessing the 'hearts and minds' of an organization to get on board with a specific change, and this requires excellent interpersonal skills and flexibility. These skills are personal rather than role-related and there is no doubt that they are innate to some people and not to others. The reality is that we could have the most highly competent Change Team with great leadership, project managers and technical experts, but if no one in the team has a naturally collaborative people focus then the change is unlikely to succeed. Collaboration breeds goodwill and trust and is, perhaps, the secret ingredient, the glue that binds everything together.

So, it's fantastic if you are reading this with the confidence that you are naturally flexible and collaborative, but that isn't going to be the case for everyone. Let's break it down into the five key skills that I believe are most important for us to master around collaboration.

The key collaborative skills

Being open-minded

The way we behave starts with our attitude. As we discussed in Chapter 4 on communication, we can't *not* communicate, because our body language is always providing clues to the way we feel about a person or situation. Therefore, we need to begin by working on our mindset. There are two aspects to this: the first is in relation to our own views and opinions about the change. Even if we don't like a change to start with, we need to understand the reasons and come to terms with the rationale for it. We need to feel genuinely open-minded about the potential positive benefits of the change and be prepared to communicate those benefits.

Secondly, and perhaps even more importantly, we need to be open-minded about the reactions and behaviours of others that we interact with when managing change. Much of this will come from our understanding about people's natural reactions to change and the way different personalities respond to change, which we will cover later. However, we can all choose our attitude towards a person or situation, even though we may not be in the habit of doing so.

If we are to be truly collaborative, we need to be open to finding a win/win outcome for both parties, even if the other person seems defensive or competitive. By being open-minded, we don't match the potentially negative reaction of the person we are aiming to collaborate with; we remain open to the best outcome for all. This takes self-discipline and patience, especially if the other person doesn't appear to be cooperating. Over time, it is likely that they will get on board, but it is important to not provide energy or reinforcement for their negative behaviour. Remember the concept of the ripple effect? This is the idea that our behaviours are like stones in a lake, creating ripples that then create additional ripples. Now, these stones and ripples could be positive or negative, i.e., they may build up or work against each other. Collaborative people effect positive ripples that build up to make a bigger difference.

Stephen Covey (1989) shares a powerful story in *The 7 Habits of Highly Effective People* that illustrates this point in completely different circumstances. He talks about the concept of a transition figure who stops the spread of negative energy even in an environment or climate that is reinforcing it. Effective Change Agents can learn to be transition figures by remaining open-minded and refusing to transmit negativity. He shares the story of a character named Stone Kyambade, who lived in a

Ugandan township and was a talented football (soccer) player in his youth. Everyone was keen to get away from the violence and poverty there and football was one of the best tickets out. Unfortunately, during a game Stone was struck down from behind by another player, resulting in a knee injury that ended his playing career and his dream of a life away from Uganda. The incident was intentional, not an accident. Now, in this environment the typical response would have been for Stone to retaliate, thus escalating into more violence. Instead, he said to the player in question, 'You did what you had to do', and that was the end of the matter.

Stone went on to coach disadvantaged children within his village to play positively with other teams and to collaborate with each other and other villages. Over time, the ripple effect was such that inter-village football became a real and positive alternative to much of the gang violence. Because Stone chose not to lower his behaviour in keeping with the environment, he stopped the transmission of negative energy. Over time, his actions sent ripples in the opposite direction, having a positive impact on his own village and many others. It is helpful to be aware of inspirational stories like this because they remind us that sometimes it is difficult to be a Change Agent, particularly in the face of adversity. By being open-minded, we can see the good in others and can stop the transmission of negative energy or resistance to change, which can sometimes be so much more powerful than positive energy. Being a Change Superhero isn't always about the transmission of positive energy; sometimes it is about choosing not to transmit negative energy.

Interpersonal awareness

If we are to be collaborative, we also need to be great at reading the behaviours of others. Just as we are communicating all the time, other people will also be displaying how they feel about a situation through their facial expressions, body language and words. Sometimes we may notice someone nod as if they agree, but their facial expression or tone of voice conveys a different message. As Change Agents we need to have the courage to spot this lack of congruence or alignment in the way others are communicating and be prepared to challenge it. Congruence is when our body language and tone of voice align to convey the same message. Incongruence is when an aspect of our communication, usually body language, tone of voice or facial expression, conveys a different message to our actual words, e.g., frowning while nodding our head as if in agreement.

If we notice incongruence in others, the way we challenge it is key, as we need to choose the right questions if we are going to get people to genuinely open up. Consider the most likely response to the following question: 'Are you sure that you are happy to go along with this?' Because it is a closed and slightly leading question, it is most likely that the individual will just answer 'Yes', rather than opening themselves up to be challenged.

So, a better interaction might be to explain the incongruence that we are seeing and then ask an open question: 'I can see you are nodding in agreement, but your facial expression gives me the impression that you are not 100% convinced that this is the right thing to do. What else should we discuss to ensure that you are completely happy?' By being specific about the behaviours that we notice, we can try not to be judgemental because our perception may be wrong. The person may respond something like: 'No, I'm on board – I am just frowning because I have the sun in my eyes', in which case we are suitably reassured, and it was good to check. Alternatively, the person may then explain their true concern, which gives us chance to address something that may have gone on to become an obstacle later.

Notice that I used a 'what' or open question, which requires more than a 'yes' or 'no' response. Unlike the previous closed question, the use of 'what' presupposes that the individual has questions, so they feel more inclined to ask them. Again, this hopefully maximizes the chances of the individual in question either sharing their concerns or convincing us further that they are on board.

Positive communication

Chapter 4 concerns the different ways in which we can communicate. When we want to be collaborative, it is essential that we communicate in a way that will be interpreted as positive. Open questions that require more than a 'yes' or 'no' response are helpful, as long as our body language gives the impression that we genuinely want to know the answer to the questions that we ask. Every question should be posed with neutral or positive tonality. This is most easily achieved by smiling as we ask a question or making sure that our internal mindset is genuinely positive or at least neutral to avoid any non-verbal 'tells'. If people start explaining their concerns then we must make sure that our body language remains open and doesn't appear defensive. This means strong eye contact and avoiding crossing our arms or legs if possible. Use of the word 'we' is powerful because it automatically creates the impression that you are both on the same team, rather than creating a position of opposition that may make people defensive.

Positive communication is also about spotting the positive behaviours of others. Collaborative people provide recognition for those demonstrating positive behaviours by sharing their story or ideas far and wide throughout the organization, making themselves visible to others. This helps inspire others to change and is a great example of the positive ripple effect that we discussed earlier.

Flexibility

Being collaborative requires us to be able to use our interpersonal awareness to spot how others are feeling and to have the flexibility to adjust our own behaviours, verbal responses or body language to build rapport and to be the most appropriate for the situation. We may need to demonstrate empathy or understanding even if we don't agree in order to gain rapport. Once we have rapport by matching the appropriate behaviours, we may be able to change the tempo or tone of communication and take the other person with us emotionally. However, we can only achieve this if we have the flexibility to notice the behaviours and match them, importantly gaining rapport and trust before we gradually adjust the tone or tempo. This is very subtle and effective if done well by a flexible communicator. Being flexible in this way isn't about manipulation or acting; it is completely genuine and people who are naturally flexible in this way are usually led by their positive intent and mindset. As with most of the skills we have outlined in this first section of the book, they can be learned or developed, but the most effective Change Agents start from within. As someone once said, 'You can't fake sincerity'. Therefore, if the intent is genuine, our behaviour will appear sincere.

Comfort with ambiguity

This is not something that comes easily to everyone, but it is a very useful Change Agent trait. During change the future becomes uncertain, which can result in people becoming blocked or unable to move forwards. We talk about different personality types in the next section of the book and people with certain traits have a marked preference for clarity and certainty over ambiguity. When faced with ambiguity they may become paralyzed or resistant as they don't understand in which direction to move. Change Agents who can create small pockets of certainty in an ambiguous situation provide reassurance, helping people to move forwards. Setting short-term goals while focusing on the here-and-now is a way of being comfortable enough with ambiguity to be able to progress in the immediate future.

Some of the best Change Agents can even interpret an ambiguous situation for others. They may be able to see through the confusion and create a vision or way forwards that others can believe in. Even if this vision may change at some point in the future, it provides positive momentum in the short term. We can learn to be more comfortable with ambiguity ourselves, even if this doesn't immediately come naturally to us, by forgiving ourselves and others when we make mistakes, by accepting that sometimes we may not get everything right and understanding that we can treat each mistake as a learning opportunity. Knowing we can change our minds makes it feel less risky to act without having the complete picture. We need to accept that we very rarely do have all the information in any situation; the key is for us to make the best decision based on the information that we do have and to be prepared to change direction in future if needed.

So, collaboration is a powerful mindset and is defined by a set of behaviours that are incredibly valuable in building relationships and delivering results during change or at any point in business. It knits together some of the behaviours discussed in previous chapters, like courage and communication, and allows us to create something bigger by including others. We can't achieve significant change on our own, so collaboration is an excellent set of skills to master.

Case study in brief: collaborating to overcome power play

Company info: a clean-energy start-up in Sierra Leone; 50 people.

Background: a solar lighting start-up was growing rapidly and was keen to offer not only ethical energy but also to promote female employment. It had a female founder and a high percentage of motivated, working women. However, attendance and morale started to drop, with stress levels rising.

Action: the management team investigated the root of the issue, assuming it was work-related. However, it found out that the issue was actually caused by the women's husbands, who were unhappy with the change in lifestyle/perceived power balance, making it hard for the women to come to work. They chose to invite the husbands to an event, to involve them in the vision and plans for the business and to recognize the contribution of their wives, acknowledging the husbands' support.

Result: almost immediately, attendance rose and stress levels decreased. The business continues to grow, with a high percentage of female employees.

Quick recap on collaboration

- Being collaborative starts with the mindset that we can achieve more together.
- Collaboration is a natural extension of great communication and social skills along with an open and honest mindset.
- Positivity of attitude and communication is a precursor to collaboration.
- Flexible interpersonal skills and comfort with ambiguity are helpful skills when collaborating.
- Recognizing and building on the positive activities of others is a powerful collaborative trait.

Online toolkit

The following free change resources can be downloaded via: www.changesuperhero.com

- The 'Five Superpowers of a Change Superhero' quiz
- The 'Five Superpowers of a Change Superhero' infographic

PART II

Change Challenges

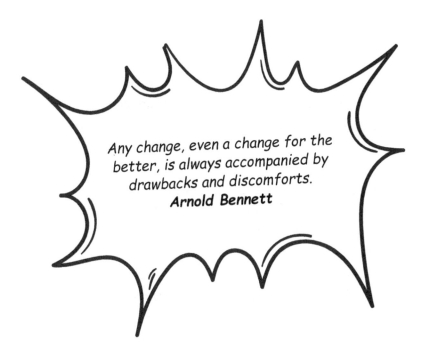

Any change, even a change for the better, is always accompanied by drawbacks and discomforts.
Arnold Bennett

Now that we have revealed the Superpowers of a Change Agent we have to identify and respond to the challenges they are going to face in the workplace. As Arnold Bennett says, all changes will also bring drawbacks or challenges. This part of the book will examine the individual's responses to change, examine how different personalities need to be managed in the change environment and highlight the role culture, values and leadership will play. Finally, we will look at the nemesis of the Change Superhero, the Culture Challenger, and look at how to ensure that change triumphs.

It is commonly stated that 70% of change initiatives fail and the cause is almost always considered to be people-related. What do we really mean by people-related? After all, most people don't come to work planning to be difficult or resistant. When we look more closely at why business change fails, there is rarely one outright change saboteur, but it is more about individual differences or cultural norms that make us fearful about change or reinforce the status quo.

This part of the book explores how we naturally respond to change in terms of both personality and emotion. We also consider the power of organizational culture, sometimes defined as 'how we do things around here'. After all, what is culture if it isn't the way groups of people operate in a habitual way, usually influenced by the environment? The challenge that this poses for our Change Superheroes is that sustainable change involves influencing both individuals and groups. We may start with just one person, but ultimately we need to encourage most people to behave in a way that may not match their personality or the environment. It is going to feel unfamiliar and perhaps uncomfortable, which means there will be significant pressure to backslide. It's like starting a new healthy eating plan but leaving all the crisps and chocolates around, providing ongoing temptation and a reminder of old eating habits.

So, for us to make lasting change, we need to be prepared to take on existing Cultural Challenges that are tempting us to behave in the old way. We need to understand how individual preferences and natural reactions to change can result in us being confronted by strange emotions, unpredictable behaviours or seemingly illogical conflicts, which might be draining and demoralizing.

The purpose of this part of the book is to point out that these human and cultural reactions to change are entirely predictable. By exposing these recognizable patterns of behaviour, it is far easier for us to consider how to counter them or – better still – use them to our advantage. This part identifies a number of predictable Change Challenges, helps us to understand their likely causes and shares tools and techniques in the following chapters that we can use to counter them.

CHAPTER 6

Individual responses to change

Paralyze resistance with persistence.
Woody Hayes

Having established that these next few chapters will look in more detail at the challenges facing the Change Superhero, this first chapter will cover the individual and will try to shed light on the role that emotion and personality play in the process, sharing some techniques that may prove useful. As the quotation suggests, resistance is a common response to change and persistence needs to be part of the Change Superhero toolkit.

One of the things that makes managing organizational change so challenging is the fact that it tends to bring out a range of emotional responses in people. If you think about it, at work we tend to try to present our best self, to be adult-like and non-emotional. This is far harder during change as emotional responses can rise to the surface and an unsuspecting Change Agent may not know how to handle them. There are a range of personality traits and factors that can influence this, some of which we will deal with in this chapter and others later in the book. The key is that the more we understand how personalities and predictable emotional responses affect individual behaviour during change, the easier it is for us to react appropriately. This in turn means that those affected by the change are more likely to buy in to the change or come to terms with it faster.

Personalities, styles and strategies

Research (Oreg, Vakola & Armenakis, 2011) shows that certain individual characteristics are likely to influence responses to change such as personality traits, individual motivational styles and coping strategies. One personality trait, known as the 'locus of control', is the extent to which individuals feel they can control or are responsible for the events that take place in their lives. If we have an internal locus of control then we have a greater sense that we can affect change ourselves, whereas people with an external locus of control tend to feel things are done to them. People with an internal locus of control have been shown to have more positive reactions to organizational change. Similarly, other studies showed that people with higher levels of self-efficacy (or self-belief) were related to greater readiness to change, engagement and commitment to change.

As Change Agents we can't control the natural locus of control or levels of self-esteem of the people we are working with, but we can, to a certain extent, predict which people may have difficulties and help them to focus on the aspects of the change that they control. Involvement in the planning and roll-out of change is a great way to help people feel more in control and therefore more positive about the change. Remember, it is not always the case that people dislike change; it is more the case that they dislike change being 'done to them'.

Organizational changes can cause stress, depression, uncertainty and insecurity (Zhou *et al.*, 2006). When it comes to stress, various factors cause it at different stages of change. Before the change, main stress factors were found to be: workload, limited resources, difficult internal or external relationships and too much or too little responsibility. During change they shifted to: internal relationships, uncertainty, unclear roles, lack of consultation/participation and the stress of others. After the change they were: workload, inadequate resources, internal relationships, continuous uncertainty and change with no perceived gain. In Part III of the book we will consider how we can communicate change and the importance of completing the cycle of change so that people appreciate actual benefits, which can help alleviate some of these stressors of change.

The transition curve

Regardless of our personality or organizational stressors, there is one helpful model that has been consistently used to explain the emotions that we all go through during change. It is known as the 'transition curve' and originated from the work of Elisabeth Kübler-Ross (1969), who studied how people coped with death and bereavement. Clearly, this is a book about organizational change; however, any change can be considered a form of loss, even a positive one. For example, if you apply for a new job and gain a promotion, there is still a sense of loss as you leave your existing role and team and move into a new one.

Kübler-Ross identified seven or eight stages and emotions that people go through during bereavement, ranging from shock and depression to integration. I am going to use an adapted version of the transition curve in this chapter that is helpful in business. There are just four stages to this journey, as can be seen in the figure below.

On the left we can see the present time, and on the far right is the future. The four stages have been labelled as denial, resistance, exploration and commitment. Depending on the perceived desirability of the change, it is possible for us to go through each stage either almost instantaneously, or at a snail's pace. It is also possible for us to move backwards and forwards along the curve. Clearly, each stage of the transition curve brings with it a set of emotions and behaviours; a point to note is that they tend to be less visible during denial and acceptance and more overt during the resistance and exploration phases.

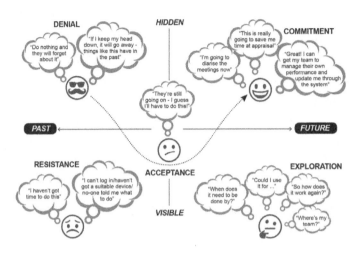

Figure 6.1 The transition curve

Of course, the goal for us as Change Agents is to help people move through the curve and reach commitment in the shortest time possible, and to stay there. When we recognize and understand the stage someone is at, we can more effectively support them through the transition curve.

Denial

The denial stage is one we often hear people referring to in relation to the personal situations of others – 'She's in denial about her husband leaving her' – or, more positively, the lottery winner stating that their win won't change them. Human beings are creatures of habit and we are drawn towards equilibrium; therefore, denial is a great way of not 'rocking the boat', and hoping that the proposed change will just go away.

Being in denial can be quite an effective strategy for those who don't like change. The reality is that many organizational changes are poorly managed and fail to become embedded, for reasons that we will discuss later. However, poor change management can mean that the cynical employee whose strategy is to just 'keep their head down' and 'wait for it all to go away' can often succeed. This is because denial is largely invisible, as opposed to the next stage of resistance. This can mean that the Change Agent mistakes silent denial for silent commitment and wrongly assumes that the individual is on board because they are not communicating otherwise.

Of course, the Change Superhero doesn't allow this to happen; they spot the possible denial and encourage the individual to express their feelings by asking specific and open questions about their views. As soon as people start talking, they begin to move on to the next stage of resistance, which may sound negative but is in fact a sign of progress.

Resistance

Once people move into resistance, they start to tell us their fears and concerns, which means we can try to address them. This can be a challenging time because it may well be quite fast-paced, frenzied and feel like conflict with people expressing anger and frustration about the situation. They will often come up with challenging questions that we may feel we should respond to, although we may not have all the answers. One of the most important aspects of this phase is for us to remember that the emotion is about the situation. We need to avoid taking it personally and becoming defensive.

People express resistance with statements like 'This will never work' or 'I've seen it all before'. These terms give us an indication of what their fears are. The key here is for us to use our empathic listening skills to truly understand their concerns and encourage the individual to continue to speak. If we appear to dismiss these concerns, the person is likely to become more vocally resistant or retreat into denial, neither of which help us to achieve our change.

The blue-bag-and-potato exercise

We need to learn to listen patiently in order to fully elicit the concerns of others. I have a long-standing colleague who uses a fantastic exercise to facilitate communication in this situation. It has the strangest name; she calls it 'the blue-bag-and-potato exercise'. I have no idea why the bag is blue, but it is purely a concept used to capture all the concerns from an individual or a group. We don't try to answer them, just gather them all, without judgement, into the imaginary blue bag. I imagine you may be wondering what the potato is for. Well, it goes in your mouth (metaphorically, of course!) to reduce the temptation to defend the change or to try to answer the concern directly. This is because we stop people from expressing their concerns as soon as we try to answer or respond, so keeping the potato in our mouth reminds us to keep quiet.

I love this as a metaphor because, although slightly crazy, it brings home the importance of letting people speak without interruption. Of course, we don't want to sit in total silence, because that is also likely to prevent people from sharing. We just need to occasionally remove the pretend potato from our mouths, in order to ask clarifying questions or to encourage further conversation. Examples might be 'Is there anything else concerning you about this change?' or 'Can you expand a little on your concerns around the changes to your working hours please?' Trying to address questions or concerns before people feel they have been fully understood is not time-efficient, even though we may think that it should be. Instead the other person is likely to disagree, argue or give more reasons why the change won't work.

What tends to happen if we continue to listen appropriately, with the odd supportive question, is that the person will start to move through the curve by themselves. We will hear them begin to ask questions that are more future-orientated even if they still appear a little hostile. They might say something like: 'Who's going to handle all the extra work caused by this change?' or 'How will I find the time to do this?' Although these are still slightly resistant questions, they are more positive and are a sign that the individual is starting to progress towards the next stage of exploration.

Exploration

Exploration is an equally vocal stage, where people interact and question the future vision looking for possibilities. We might hear more questions around possibilities, like 'Will I get a pay rise?' or 'What new roles will be available?', which allow us to interact more naturally (and take the potato out of our mouth). The main difference between resistance and exploration is the fact that the individual is clearly starting to picture what the future will look like after the change has taken place, which means they are spending more time on the right-hand side of the curve. It is perfectly normal for them to move backwards and forwards between resistance and exploration and this is when we can start to answer some of the questions or concerns raised. Remember, we don't have to know all the answers at the time; what we need to do is understand the concerns fully. It is then perfectly OK to say that you are going to take the issues away in order to get full answers. We are then able to group concerns together, use them to inform future communication and provide more comprehensive answers.

The interesting thing about this exercise is that we might do this in a one-to-one or a one-to-many situation; it is the act of allowing people to express their views and concerns in a safe non-judgemental way that helps them to process the change. Even without the answers we are helping them to come to terms with the change – just like the grieving process.

Some people will naturally move from exploration to commitment on their own as they visualize and process the future vision, particularly if they believe it to be positive. However, there will be some who remain stuck at an earlier stage, even when we have answered their concerns to the best of our ability. We then need to stand firm, explain the expectations and be clear that the change is here to stay. We should share success stories of how it has worked for other people (think of Chapter 3 on influencing through persuasion) but ultimately they need to realize that the change is not optional.

You can see in Figure 6.2 the different ways in which we can help people through each stage of the transition curve.

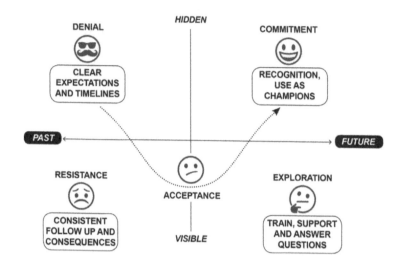

Figure 6.2 How to manage each stage

Commitment

The interesting thing about people who have reached the commitment stage is that it is almost silent; the frantic questions cease and the energy becomes quieter and more channelled. If we have witnessed someone going through all four stages, then it is obvious when they have reached commitment.

However, as mentioned before, we mustn't mistake the quietness of denial for the quietness of commitment. It is easy to check by asking a few questions about how they feel about the change. If we get a quick and positive answer, then they have reached commitment. On the other hand, if they take a deep breath and give a textbook answer or their body language appears incongruent then we may need to ask a few follow-up questions to be truly sure that they are on board.

We all go through these predictable stages during change, some of us quickly and some of us more slowly. Ultimately, if we are to be successful in delivering change then we must take as many people with us, as quickly as possible. People who have made it through the Change Curve and reached commitment are in a great position to help others through the same journey. They may become our First Followers, early adopters or champions – all key roles during organizational change.

One of the worst things that can happen is if people 'quit and stay', as in, they don't buy in to the change but they don't choose to vote with their feet and leave. In organizations where successive changes have taken place but haven't been driven through to completion there can be a high proportion of people who fit into this category, creating a culture of resistance and stagnation. This makes future changes extremely difficult. Starting by understanding each individual, one at a time, the Change Superhero can unblock stagnant cultures, increasing the chances of a successful change outcome.

Case study in brief: the transition curve in business

Company info: UK technology firm; 200 people.

Background: the CEO requested a data protection audit from an external consultant. He was the named chief data officer and stated how confident he was about the results. The consultant carried out the audit and found a number of issues, which she documented in a 25-page report she provided to the CEO via email before a follow-up phone call.

Situation: the CEO initially didn't accept the findings (denial) and then started to argue about the findings (resistance), saying things like 'That's not true' and 'Who told you that?' Occasionally he would ask questions like 'What if we interpreted it like this?', and the conversation finished with him concerned about the impact of the findings on the business investment.

Result: the consultant empathized with the CEO's concerns and coached him through ideas and solutions to close the gaps in the report. She suggested that the report could be used as evidence of the firm's commitment to data protection and viewed positively; 12 months later, the CEO invited her back for a follow-up audit. All the previous issues had been dealt with and the firm was held up as a role-model business (commitment).

Quick recap on individual responses to change

- Individuals go through a predictable set of emotions akin to grief during change.
- We experience the same emotions, regardless of whether it is positive or negative change.
- The pace at which we go through the Change Curve will vary from person to person.
- It is possible to go backwards as well as forwards through the Change Curve.
- Resistance to change is a healthy part of the journey and shouldn't be mistaken for negativity.

Online toolkit

The following free change resources can be downloaded via: www.changesuperhero.com

- 'Transition Curve' PowerPoint presentation

CHAPTER 7

Personality and change

> *No type has everything. The introverts and thinkers, though likely to arrive at the most profound decisions, may have the most difficulty in getting their conclusions accepted. The opposite types are best at communicating, but not as adept at determining the truths to be communicated.*
>
> **Isabel Briggs Myers**

The purpose of this chapter is to share a fundamental understanding of the role personality plays in our response to change and how we as Change Superheroes need to balance the different needs of the different personality types and traits to keep the process on track for success.

Most of us would agree that everyone is unique to some degree and personalities vary. This means that our individual responses to change are likely to vary too, and there are a range of personality tools available that can be used to understand these individual differences. For every lover of a personality tool, there will also be a critic who doesn't like to be pigeonholed or believes the tool isn't well researched. I'm of the view that any theory or tool that helps us to understand how our preferences or behaviours may differ from those of others can be useful, as long as we engage with an open mind. This is because individual differences or personalities can often cause misunderstanding or conflict, particularly during change. Therefore, any framework that helps us to avoid misunderstanding and build relationships is going to be useful, particularly in highly charged, emotional environments such as those during change.

Type or trait

In psychology, individual differences or personality can be measured in terms of different 'types' or 'traits'. Personality types are defined by binary dimensions – so people would be classified as one of two opposite types: introverted or extroverted, for example. Type theory can be criticized because people often dislike being pigeonholed into one of two camps and may believe that they exhibit different behaviours in different environments or are able to demonstrate both types equally. Trait theories measure the extent to which we demonstrate a certain personality type or behaviour.

Extroversion can also be measured on a scale, as a personality trait. Whether we prefer type or trait theory, the key is using the right tool for the right purpose. For recruitment or focused one-to-one development, I would recommend a personality trait tool because it can be explored in detail. However, when we are in group situations like managing organizational change or working with teams, an awareness and application of personality types can be helpful. This is due to the simplicity of a more binary approach, which helps us to deliver change in a way that is appropriate to most types and therefore likely to appeal to all.

Myers–Briggs type indicator

To further illustrate this point in our context of change, I am going to focus on the Myers–Briggs Type Indicator (MBTI) in this chapter. It was published in the 1960s based on work carried out by mother-and-daughter duo Katharine Cook Briggs and her daughter, Isabel Briggs Myers (Myers, 1995). The origins can be traced back to original research by psychologist Carl Jung in the 1920s and Briggs and Myers developed it over 40 years. Since then, MBTI has been further researched and developed by what is now known as the Myers-Briggs Company, and is very popular.

MBTI uses four different dimensions of type, which are referred to by single letters. These dichotomies are classified as follows:

- where you focus your attention – extroversion (E) or introversion (I)
- how you take in information – sensing (S) or intuition (N)

- how you make decisions – thinking (T) or feeling (F)
- how you deal with the world – judging (J) or perceiving (P)

No single type is superior overall, although each one has different strengths that are helpful in different situations. If we were using MBTI in a one-to-one, we would group the dimensions together to give someone a four-letter type, e.g., ENTP or ISTJ. However, that is far too complicated for our purpose, which is first about understanding more generally how people respond to and process change and, second, being able to explain change in a way that is helpful to most types.

Extroversion or introversion

Let's understand each dimension in turn and consider how to recognize or respond to these during change. So, extroversion and introversion can often, but not always, be recognized by how expressive someone is about their internal thoughts. An analogy worth considering is the difference between push and pull data on your phone inbox. The opinion of an extroverted personality is almost like data that is continually being pushed to a phone's inbox (or out of their mouth!). There is practically no delay in accessing their viewpoint if you seek it. On the other hand, an introvert represents more of a pull approach to data synchronization; there may be a slight delay while they go inside (to the server) and synchronize. When they do respond, it is much more likely to be a fully thought through and reliable response.

What does this mean for us as Change Agents? Well, if we think back to the transition curve from the last chapter, then it is likely that extroverts are going to express their feelings about change sooner than introverts. It is likely that we will have a disproportionately high level of views from the extroverts, who are more likely to express their feelings voluntarily, than we do from the introverts. This could result in a distorted view.

So, an introvert may be in the resistance stage of the transition curve in their head but may not express it. The risk could be that we hear extroverts talking excitedly about the future and assume that everybody is on board. Extroverts can be very vocal and dominant and in an emotive environment of change this could mean that we only get to hear their side of the story; the introverts are not going to push themselves forward. Fundamentally, to be successful in helping everyone to process change effectively, we have to communicate in ways that allow both types to be heard.

This means accepting that introverts may take longer to process information and longer to share how they feel, and we need to create safe environments that allow them to do that. Processes like the blue-bag-and-potato exercise use a structured way of eliciting concerns from a group and may be helpful. If we imagine sitting around the table, we would go to each person in turn, asking for their thoughts and concerns, which would give both introverts and extroverts a fair hearing. The method of capturing all the thoughts in the bag rather than responding directly allows the manager or Change Agent to digest the concerns, preventing an extroverted 'off-the-cuff' and possibly unhelpful response. If the Change Agent is more introverted, it also gives them chance to reflect and give a considered response.

Sensing or intuition

So, having considered the impact of extroversion and introversion, the next MBTI type concerns how we take in information, via either sensing or intuition. A sensing preference is characterized by a preference for more practical, detailed processes, whereas intuition is more vague, futuristic and 'big-picture'. If we consider these differences in relation to change then we could theorize that someone with an intuition preference might be predisposed to change as they seek it out and are attracted to it. If this is correct, then those with an intuition preference are likely to accelerate through the transition curve into commitment ahead of those around them. If accurate, then we can encourage people like this to be great Change Agents in their own right.

On the other hand, someone with a sensing preference is going to require lots of structured information. They will want to understand the process step-by-step before they can move forwards. So, if we think back to the transition curve, these are the sort of people who may seem to be stuck at the resistance stage because they are questioning all the facts. But when we realize this is just how they process the world, and provide them with the detail they need, then they will happily move on.

Thinking or feeling

The third dichotomy is about how we make decisions, either by thinking or feeling. If I have a thinking preference, then I base my decisions on facts and logic and am less likely to involve emotion in this process. If I understand the logical argument for a change then I am likely to just accept it. Someone with a thinking preference presented with a potentially emotive change like redundancy is likely to just accept it, if supported by a logical rationale. Their focus will be on the practical realities such as timings and redundancy packages as opposed to how they feel about it.

On the other hand, someone with a feeling preference makes decisions based on values and feelings. In the same situation they will often be concerned for other people, not just themselves, and may appear quite emotional. They may start asking questions on behalf of others, which may not even be their own concerns.

Obviously as Change Agents we need to respond appropriately to both these styles and should have thought through the logical argument, treating people fairly in any change situation. However, this preference can also make a difference in those delivering or managing the change. A Change Agent with a thinking preference may be very matter-of-fact about change, which could appear cold. On the other hand, someone delivering change with a feeling preference may empathize too much and bring too much emotion to their communication. Both risks can be avoided with self-awareness.

Judging or perceiving

The final set of MBTI preferences concerns judging or perceiving, described as 'How we like to live our lives', which is rather general. It is important to understand that judging doesn't mean being judgemental in this context – it actually means that people like closure. Those with a judging preference like to make decisions and have plans and structures agreed. They also like to have time to plan, and don't appreciate last-minute changes. Changes to carefully thought-out plans can be highly stressful to a person with a judging preference. Having said that, once they have had time to come to terms with the change, they are likely to achieve closure and accept the change as a new reality.

People with a perceiving preference, on the other hand, are always open to new experiences; they like to leave their options open, are flexible and tend to see a change of plan as an opportunity. They seek out change and are likely to move quickly through the transformation curve to the exploration stage, looking for the positives that the change may bring. They can be helpful to others by spotting the positives in change and helping others to come to terms with it. In my experience, people with a perceiving preference are also likely to be natural Change Agents.

There are many other different personality tools available that can also be applied to change in order to provide equally helpful insights. The tool doesn't really matter; what matters is our ability to recognize how different personality types are predisposed to change. This helps us to understand different reactions to change and to plan our communication in ways that are likely to appeal to the majority. Remember that our own personality type will play a part in the way we respond to and communicate change as well. Appreciating how our preferences may differ from those of others gives us insight into the experiences and realities of others. Delivering change effectively requires us to take the majority with us and understanding and adapting to individual difference is another way of doing this.

Case study in brief: understanding how different personalities respond to change

Company info: a children's nursery; 50 people.

Background: the nursery was taken over by new owners, who wanted to improve the way it operated and ultimately improve profitability. The original manager departed, leaving two team leaders who needed to take over the changes, with the support of an HR consultant. The team leaders had very different personalities and didn't appear to work particularly well together, which was sending mixed messages to parents and staff.

Action: the HR consultant noticed that team leader A was quite withdrawn and very serious, only asking questions about the specific requirements of the new role, processes and time frames (potential ISTJ personality profile). Team leader B was talkative but erratic, a little emotional and easily distracted (potential ENFP personality profile). She realized that the individuals probably had opposite MBTI types and were responding differently to the stress of change. She provided them with an understanding of their relative strengths and preferences and helped them to see the benefit of working with their opposite type.

Result: the two team leaders worked collaboratively to change the way the nursery operated, with team leader A managing systems, processes and finance and team leader B focusing on staff, customers and marketing. In time, one became the overall manager with the other as deputy and both continued to work collaboratively 12 months later.

Quick recap on personality and change

- Different personalities will respond differently to change.
- Change Agents need to appreciate these differences and flex their style accordingly.
- Certain personality traits may make people natural Change Agents.
- Our own preferences may bring bias to the way we communicate change.
- It doesn't matter which personality tool we use; the key is appealing to the majority.

Online toolkit

The following free change resources can be downloaded via: www.changesuperhero.com
- MBTI and change overview

CHAPTER 8

Culture, values and leadership

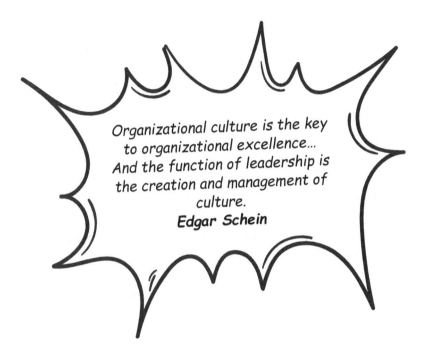

Organizational culture is the key to organizational excellence... And the function of leadership is the creation and management of culture.
Edgar Schein

Much of our focus so far has been on the individual Change Agent. We have considered the skills and personal traits of the individual during change but haven't yet considered the impact of organizational culture. This has such a powerful impact on the success of any initiative that people will often cite it as being the leading cause of change failing. Therefore, however well thought out the technical and project-related aspects of change, we can still encounter insurmountable resistance if we don't address the cultural aspects of change. To help us do this, we need to be able to conceptualize the prevailing culture, despite it being a nebulous concept. We will start with a definition and then explore some cultural models, including those defined by Edgar Schein (quoted above), which we can use as a reference point for our own cultural change. Schein is clear that leadership and culture are intrinsically linked (2004) and we go on to explore these views, along with looking at a selection of cultural models that we can use as reference points for our own cultural change.

Defining culture

While researching this book, I was struck by how many definitions for culture there were. Here is a small selection.

> It is the collective programming of the mind which distinguishes the members of one group or category of people from another.
>
> (Hofstede, 1994)

> Culture is a fuzzy set of basic assumptions and values, orientations to life, beliefs, policies, procedures and behavioural conventions that are shared by a group of people, and that influence (but do not determine) each member's behaviour and his/her interpretations of the 'meaning' of other people's behaviour.
>
> (Spencer-Oatey & Franklin, 2009)

'How we do things around here' is a commonly used shortcut for culture, usually attributed to Charles Handy

(1981). This statement emphasizes the unconscious and unspoken aspects of culture, illustrating how deep-rooted and therefore potentially hard to change it is.

Cultural models

The first model that we will explore is Edgar Schein's (1984) 'Onion Model'. He originally divided culture into three different levels: artefacts and symbols, espoused values and basic underlying assumptions. I have adapted the model here to show how closely interlinked leadership and values are when it comes to recognizing culture.

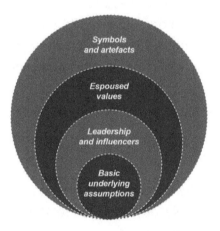

Figure 8.1 The 'Onion Model'

Symbols and artefacts

The outside layer of culture is demonstrated through symbols and artefacts. These are visible to the outside world but are just the tip of the iceberg. They are things like logos, branding, corporate offices, job titles, hierarchies and some processes. Formal examples may be recognition schemes or a company website. Less formal examples may be the way people dress or communicate when making decisions.

The modern symbols and artefacts of many of the highly successful software firms in Silicon Valley, such as bright décor, beanbags and pool tables, are synonymous with a young, innovative culture. Other companies have introduced similar features in the hope of emulating the success of these businesses, only to realize that they are just symbols of the culture, not the cause. Simply changing a logo or brand or making other symbolic changes is not the same as actual culture change, which needs to originate from within the deeper layers of an organization. When we dig beneath the surface of these highly successful businesses, we should find that it is the leadership behaviours and espoused values of the company that drive the creativity and innovation rather than the table football or indoor deckchairs.

Espoused values

This leads to the second level, the 'espoused values' of a company. Simply put, values are the core beliefs and commitments that provide the foundation to the way a company conducts business. The reality is that every company has values, even if they aren't written on the wall. They are recognizable through the behaviours that are demonstrated daily and are particularly visible in the actions of leaders and key influencers.

Sometimes these values are baked into the company from the start by the founders. Elsewhere, they evolve over time as the company grows and differentiates itself from the competition. Values should be the bedrock of a company's culture. They can establish behavioural standards and help employees to understand the best decision to make in the absence of guidance. As a company grows, core values can help it manage change without compromising the factors that have made it successful. The processes, activities and metrics used on a regular basis will also become representative of the culture and values. Many of these mechanisms may represent the style of past leaders or may have been established in response to historic market forces or events. It is important that we remember to change these to be reflective of the culture we aspire to, rather than the culture we used to have. Schein calls them primary embedding mechanisms:

- what we measure on a regular basis – think dashboards and KPIs
- the way emergencies or critical incidents are handled
- the way resources are allocated
- the behaviours that are role-modelled, recognized and encouraged by leaders
- the allocation of reward and promotion

Leadership and influencers

The behaviours of key leaders, espoused values and symbols are interlinked layers of an organizational culture and it is unlikely we will change one without affecting the other. Of course, this means that many values-based change initiatives are received with cynicism, particularly if they are perceived to be imposed from the top down or leaders are seen as paying 'lip service' to them. The bottom line is that the behaviours of the leaders and managers will reinforce or undermine any defined values and in turn make or break any culture change.

Consider the example of a sales organization within a business with an outspoken and charismatic sales director. He has established a well-known but generally unspoken cultural rule that men in sales have to wear a suit and tie in the office, and not only that – the shirt must be white. Females must also be 'suited and booted'. As you would expect, the sales director always dresses this way and while he cannot demand that others do the same, he ridicules anyone who steps out of this norm. It is a powerful symbol of the sales culture. No matter how many times people try to introduce 'dress-down Fridays' or informal dress codes, those who want to get on in the sales organization emulate the dress of this individual.

Basic underlying assumptions

According to the Onion Model, the deepest level of culture is the basic underlying assumptions of an organization, which are generally unconscious behaviours or beliefs. They tend to be so deep-rooted that they are hard to recognize from within the organization or in an individual, but new starters may find them noticeable. Take the example of someone joining a start-up from a long-standing corporate role. In their interview they may have been assured of full training and support to guide them through induction. Their expectations are based on their corporate background and they might expect a formal training and induction programme. However, the start-up mentality is one of self-sufficiency. People are happy to help but there is an assumption that the learning will be on-the-job, informal and owned by the individual. Depending on the aptitude of the new starter, this may or may not be a great fit for them personally, and is an example of the importance of recruiting for attitudes and beliefs that are a good fit with company culture.

Takeaways

So, what are the key takeaways for us as Change Agents in relation to Schein's model? Fundamentally, the principle should be to make change from the inside out, rather than the outside in. Basic assumptions may be too deep-rooted to change, but leadership and values are a better place to start. It is only after we have got the leadership on board and the values aligned that making symbolic changes is worthwhile. These should be the finishing touches rather than the starting point.

However, although leadership behaviours and values are intrinsically linked to culture, this isn't the only place to start if we want to change a culture. In fact, some experts believe that we shouldn't focus on culture change as an end in itself. Instead, we should start with the business strategy or problem, align the values and allow the culture change to develop from there. The logic here is that the business need is likely to provide the all-important motivation for behaviours to change.

After all, an organization's culture will almost certainly have developed over time, possibly as a response to external market forces. Consider the PESTLE forces: political, economic, social, technological, legal and environmental. A business may have developed a culture of being fast-moving and innovative to take advantage of technology, allowing it to enter a new economic market. On the other hand, a business in a very highly regulated marketplace may appear to be risk-averse and focused on quality. If market forces change, we may need to behave in ways that are counter to our culture in order to be more competitive. We talked about connecting with strategy earlier. Making the link with market forces helps everyone to understand why the change is necessary and motivates people to move in a new direction.

The Competing Values Framework

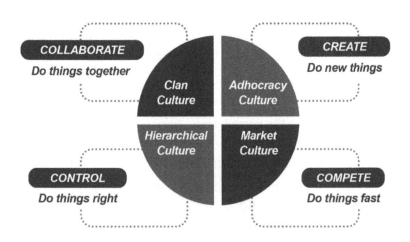

Figure 8.2 Competing Values Framework

From their research into what makes organizations effective, Robert Quinn and Kim Cameron came up with the Competing Values Framework (CVF) (Quinn & Cameron, 2006). They identified two dimensions: flexibility versus stability, and internal versus external orientation, which resulted in four quadrants with distinctly different corporate cultures, as shown in Figure 8.2.

Clan culture

As the name suggests, the value here is about doing things together. The culture is built on personal relationships or loyalty, particularly to the founder or clan leader. The company may be referred to as having a 'family feel', which may be positive, although like a family there can be infighting and bickering too. In addition to the value of 'doing things together' the organizational values are likely to be disproportionately affected by the personal values or behavioural style of the founder or family. While these values are appropriate to the marketplace the culture will work, but it can be problematic as the company grows. Think of start-ups, family businesses or small ICT companies. When founder- or family-led businesses want to scale up or sell, the clan culture can become the sticking point, unless the clan leader is able to model and embed new, more appropriate values.

Our role as Change Agents here is to hold a mirror up to the clan leader's behaviours if they aren't supporting the new way of working. We may need to help bring in new leadership roles or establish more formal processes and ways of working. Sometimes, the best option is for the clan leader to move on if they can't take on a less influential role.

Hierarchical culture

On the other hand, hierarchical cultures are formal and structured with embedded processes and procedures and little room for flexibility. The prevailing values are 'do things right' and 'follow the rules' because these provide stability and control, resulting in quality and efficiency. The challenge for this culture is speed to adapt to change. For example, a competitor may disrupt the marketplace, generating a requirement for innovation or cost savings. Risk-averse, hierarchical cultures can be slow to change, which could ultimately affect their ability to survive. There are many manufacturing and retail examples of this culture failing when the market changes. The hierarchical businesses that do well are those that manage to 'bake in' innovation as part of their processes and values, e.g., large German engineering companies and Japanese car manufacturers. Admittedly, they often have deep pockets and retained profits, which means they may be able to survive cultural evolution rather than revolution, whereas younger companies may not.

Our role as Change Agents in a hierarchical culture is about rolling out textbook-style change. We need to plan and communicate the change well, enlist a league of fellow Change Agents in support and should ensure that realistic timelines are set for the delivery of change.

Market culture

These businesses will say they are customer-focused; however, this is more of a means to an end. The real value in a market culture is winning or beating the competition. This sort of culture is predominantly externally focused, which means that employees can feel like an afterthought or a means to an end. Market cultures are focused on goals, results and clearly align themselves with the external marketplace.

They aim to predict and respond to customer needs in order to beat the competition, achieve profitability and market dominance. Customer retention and satisfaction are terms that all employees are aware of and potentially measured against. Change in this culture needs to be strongly aligned with the company strategy, potentially highlighting the relationship between employee wellbeing and customer satisfaction. It is likely that the culture is set by a handful of key influencers, particularly in sales and marketing, so winning over key individuals for any culture change will be essential.

Adhocracy culture

These businesses are also externally focused, but they focus on winning new business through innovation and creativity. We often hear the term 'disruptive' being applied to businesses that are shaking up traditional marketplaces through innovation. They may be winning business from traditional hierarchical cultures or they may be creating new markets. They value creativity and speed to market, which means the management style needs to be empowering so that people feel able to take the initiative.

Power is again likely to be dispersed in these cultures and it may not necessarily sit with those who are most senior. Individuals with key technical skills can be extremely powerful and change can be initiated or resisted from anywhere in the organization. Because this culture is so individualistic, we have to take everyone with us during change, which means our communication needs to be widespread and extremely influential.

It is possible to obtain a cultural questionnaire for the CVF, which can be used to diagnose the current cultural position of the leadership of an organization. In planned change work this can be a helpful tool.

The Cultural Web

We will explore one final model of culture, Johnson, Scholes and Whittington's Cultural Web (1999), because it is a helpful model for planning our future desired culture. At the core of the web is the organizational paradigm: the core values, mindset or motivation of the organization. One of the four cultural types outlined above could fit into this centre point, giving us a cultural perspective to look through. This is surrounded and supported by six cultural influences.

Figure 8.3 The Cultural Web

- **Organizational structures**. These refer to the hierarchy of the organization and will illustrate where the power lies, how decisions are made and where communication flows.

- **Control systems**. The systems and mechanisms that report on and control the organization. What we measure tends to drive behaviour.
- **Power structures**. These are the people and systems that have power and influence and can get things done, with both formal positional power and informal personal power.
- **Symbols**. The official and unofficial visual representations of culture, e.g., logos, offices, uniforms.
- **Stories and myths**. Past events and stories about the organization and its people that continue to be shared both internally and externally.
- **Rituals and routines**. The habitual activities, norms and ways of working.

What is nice about this model is the way in which we can use it to analyze our current culture – 'as is' – and to help define the culture that is 'to be'. This helps provide clarity about the required change, both structural and cultural, which helps us decide what changes need to be made to embed it.

Table 8.1 An example of a Cultural Web

	As is	To be
Organizational paradigm	Financially stable, trustworthy, quality- and research-driven	Innovative, responsive, customer-focused
Organizational structures	Hierarchical roles with formal reporting into a parent company	Matrix or team-based structures focused around market requirements

Control systems	Board of directors and non-execs make decisions. Formal annual cycles of budgeting, headcount and objective cascade	Disseminated decision-making and financial controls and business-case-driven resourcing and budgeting
Power structures	CEO and CFO and influence of the parent company	Individual empowerment and accountability with local team leaders and managers
Symbols	Traditional brand and logo, parking spaces for top execs, status related to size of office and formal business attire at work	Open-plan buildings, hot desks, 'chill-out zones' and online collaboration tools
Rituals and routines	Annual business planning, board meetings, sales conferences, annual reports and long-service awards	Team huddles, weekly one-to-ones, informal Skype chats and fish-and-chip Fridays
Stories and myths	The CFO values the company car fleet above people, there is gossip about the executive board and board meetings never finish on time	Reward and recognition linked to customer impact, innovation suggestion schemes and individual success stories

You can download a template of the above Cultural Web analysis from our online toolkit (see below) and use it to analyze the 'as is' and 'to be' culture of your own organization. You can then consider the changes that are required in each area to deliver the desired change.

Culture is one of our biggest Change Challenges. This is because it is multifaceted and so tightly interwoven with leadership, values and behaviours. Change will only occur if we adjust enough of the many variables and align leadership behaviours against them for long enough. However, once the culture has shifted, the change is here to stay.

Case study in brief: using vision and values as a catalyst for cultural change

Company info: a healthcare business; 300 people.

Background: a new business was created as a result of a management buyout from a global market leader. The prevalent cultural norms were around top-down decision-making with a tendency for a blame culture. The new leadership team needed to make the company easier to do business with and realized that a culture change was needed.

Action: the executive team agreed on a common set of visions and values that were translated into and aligned with their code of conduct, providing clear expectations of aligned behaviours that were consistently reinforced through good people management. Those demonstrating the values were publicly recognized for doing things right and, over time, consequences and repercussions were implemented for those who weren't.

Result: change was gradual; however, within three to five years the new culture was fully embedded. There was higher engagement and accountability and increased customer confidence. The business gained financial security and was outstripping competitors at tender, driving rapid growth.

Quick recap on culture, values and leadership

- Culture, values and leadership are all intrinsically linked when it comes to change.
- There is no point in changing cultural symbols and expecting it to result in change.
- Leadership behaviours are the strongest manifestation of organizational values.
- Focus on business need for change rather than culture change as the objective.
- When we understand the paradigm of the organization, we can choose the best approach to make change.

Online toolkit

The following free change resources can be downloaded via: www.changesuperhero.com
- Cultural Web template

CHAPTER 9

Cultural Challenges

Change has its enemies.
Robert Kennedy

In the previous chapters we have shown that we can plan change carefully, considering the organizational culture and the different personality types within it. However, we can still get ambushed by Cultural Challenges or enemies when we least expect it. This chapter reveals some of the most common ones and provides suggestions how our Change Superhero can best disarm them.

Understanding conflict

We should start by understanding our own relationship with conflict; we all have different reactions to it and some of us try hard to avoid it. The reality is that delivering change is unlikely to come without some level of conflict, so we may as well be prepared. The word conflict often conjures up thoughts of angry, raised voices with overt challenge, which can be intimidating for many. However, there is also a more insidious type of conflict that can be just as challenging and possibly more damaging if not addressed. This is covert conflict, whereby people don't air their concerns openly. They may come over as being passive-aggressive or nod in agreement to our faces but then do nothing or talk negatively behind our back. We need to be prepared to build the skills to manage both overt and covert conflict if needed and will need to unleash our communication Superpowers to do this.

Overt conflict

As outlined earlier, overt conflict is visible; it is when people display emotions, and we might recognize this as resistance when people are experiencing change. There can also be other fundamental reasons for overt conflict like fear, lack of understanding or the other person just having a bad day. Whatever the cause, the solution is the same – we must listen and show sincere empathy for the emotions being displayed. Note the importance of the word sincere here, because we have probably all experienced call-centre staff whose empathy comes over as patronizing, simply adding fuel to our frustrations. Sincere, empathic listening involves eye contact, nodding, a sympathetic facial expression and occasional reflective statements. These might be phrases like 'I am sorry to hear this' or 'That sounds like a big concern to you' or 'That must have been extremely frustrating'. Remember, the goal is to make the other person feel understood and we know that we have achieved this when their response to our reflective statement is an impassioned 'yes'. This is the point at which trust is built, making people far more open to our views or recommendations. Having established trust, we can then utilize another of our Superpowers and use courage to make our case.

Covert conflict

Courage is also required when we are dealing with covert conflict. This may be hard to spot, and we need to be alert to the body language of others. We might recognize incongruent body language where someone agrees to a change or action but their facial expression doesn't align with the spoken words. They may demonstrate a blank facial expression, quietly shake their heads or shrug when you are delivering a message. We might notice them mouthing words under their breath or whispering to someone next to them. It is very easy to ignore or overlook these behaviours, particularly if we would rather avoid direct conflict personally. Unfortunately, this can result in the spread of negativity and resistance to the change that we are trying to engender. To deal with covert conflict, we need to be prepared to challenge the behaviours calmly and constructively. Again, our tone of voice and facial expression needs to be curious rather than combative. So we might say something like 'I noticed that you seemed to say something under your breath just then;

do you have some thoughts or concerns that you would like to raise?' or 'All views are valid and welcome; what are your thoughts on this suggestion?' or 'I can't help feeling that you may have some reservations; would you be prepared to share them?' Usually, the individual will be taken aback but will share their concerns or issues and you will be able to address them. Occasionally they will be slightly startled and state that there is no problem. This is your opportunity to reinforce the fact that you are open to all views and that the change is here to stay, so it is important that everyone is on board. Although this individual is unlikely to be your strongest advocate, it should prevent them from undermining your project.

Six types of Cultural Challenges

Now we are in a position to address individual conflict, it is worth looking at other covert Cultural Challenges that can undermine change if we are not prepared for it. They can be caused by specific individuals, subgroups or cultural norms. Whatever the cause, it is worth us being able to recognize some of these common blockers to change. Here are a few examples that you may have come across and ideas on how to combat them.

A 'no' culture

This is the sort of organizational culture that may overvalue critical analysis to such an extent that almost anyone can say 'no' to change but hardly anyone can say 'yes'. Many of us have experienced organizations filled with cynics and critics who can always find a good reason not to do something.

Pushing back and resisting change by being critical is an easy way to avoid taking risks. If we can understand the root of the issue, then we can be better prepared to deal with this kind of challenge. We can prepare our business case complete with full analysis of the risks and potential benefits of the change. When presenting our message, we can pre-empt some of the likely perceived risks by explaining how we have considered these and have risk mitigation in place. We need to remove the fear and make it easy for people to say 'yes'. Often, introducing a change project as a trial, pilot or proof of concept makes it easier to overcome the 'no' culture.

Not-invented-here-itis

This is similar to the 'no' culture in that people push back on any change, almost automatically and without real consideration. It can be really frustrating for the Change Agent, who might feel rejected without any logical answer or fair hearing. Again, certain people tend to be more likely to act like this than others and some may say it is also about fear or insecurity. Whatever the cause, the most effective way of overcoming this Cultural Challenger is by involvement. Identify the people most likely to block the change early and get their input. If you can, take a suggestion or quote from them and incorporate it into the plan or change messaging. In other words, make them feel like they played a key part in developing the change or even that it was their idea in the first place.

Playing the game

This is when any decision, however small, must be turned into a detailed board paper and signed off by the executive team.

It is particularly common in bureaucratic organizations and is probably driven by a combination of lack of confidence by those at the top and an institutionalized mindset. Often, it seems that the purpose is about creating an audit trail of data that will protect the ultimate decision-makers in future, should their decisions be questioned.

This type of environment can be exhausting for the well-meaning Change Agent as they eagerly knock over the various barriers and hurdles in the pursuit of getting a decision made, only to have their paper discarded at the last minute. These cultures are very difficult to change and require a combination of being seen to 'play the game' by writing the paper and gaining sponsorship from the most influential person at the top of the organization. It is sad to say, but it is also the type of culture where Change Agents should be selective in the changes that they get involved in and only choose those with strong sponsorship. If you are going to prepare a board paper, why not try a PowerPoint or a summary 'one-pager'? This still creates an audit trail but can get your point across faster. It is also worth booking one-to-one, face-to-face meetings with those at the top table before you present your paper, if you are to be confident of keeping it on the agenda and gaining support.

Keeping up with the Joneses

This kind of culture reflects a perceived competitiveness in the marketplace, where there is a constant focus on what others are doing. This is sometimes indicative of a 'me-too' marketplace where there is little to differentiate one product or company from others, reflecting a lack of confidence in the market position or strategy by the leadership. The tendency here is to avoid making decisions unless others are seen to be doing the same thing. Obviously, the best way to get decisions or support for change here is to use the competition as a reference point for your business case. Give examples or case studies of how others have made the same decisions and had brilliant results. Try creating urgency around potential resource shortage or likely competitor behaviour.

After the meeting ends, debate begins

This links to our conversation on conflict, where on the surface people are smiling and pleasant about our plan, but the real debate only takes place behind the scenes. Often, this is down to one very dominant or powerful individual who others don't feel able to challenge. Like covert conflict, this is difficult to address if it is invisible. As Change Agents we need to be able to identify where this is happening and bring it to the surface, otherwise we end up with very political situations where decisions are made behind closed doors and meetings and collaboration create cynicism because they constitute an empty ritual.

If this is the culture around the board table and we are relatively junior Change Agents, there is very little we can do personally. Perhaps we can raise this with human resources, who might set the scene for some executive coaching or board development by bringing in a neutral facilitator who can build trust and promote insight. Once the team are open to being more effective, the facilitator can work with them to uncover rules and codes of conduct. This is likely to take some time but should result in people expressing their views on future change more openly.

Keep your head down and it will go away

Many organizations have experienced a succession of change initiatives, many of which have not been completed. Even when initially proclaimed as urgent, the direction might have shifted and the change simply didn't happen. Perhaps the business requirement changed, or the leadership simply didn't manage the change through to completion. Whatever the cause, the result tends to be jaded employees who will react to the next change with cynicism, whatever it is. The real challenge for the Change Agent is convincing these cynics that this time the change is for real. There are three ways of aiming to achieve this; first, plan your change really well, think about potential obstacles and how to overcome them up front. The second point is to acknowledge that previous changes haven't been completed, but communicate clearly that this one is here to stay, with firm backing from a credible sponsor. Finally, ensure that the change is followed through to completion.

Conclusion

In conclusion of Part II of this book, we can see that this chapter has raised some of the more nuanced challengers to change. In the case of overt conflict we will almost certainly notice the challenge and our response will vary according to our level of comfort with conflict. However, covert conflict and many of the Cultural Challenges outlined above are more insidious and easier to avoid than they are to address.

Drawing attention to Cultural Challenges gives us the choice to utilize our Change Superpowers from the first part of the book and influence a better outcome for all. Combining these skills with our awareness of potential challenges puts us in a better position to plan for change rather than just react to it.

The next section shows us how we might 'save the world' by building a Change Master Plan. We consider how to plan, manage and communicate change effectively. Many of the Cultural Challenges above are caused by failed historic changes that weren't seen through to the end. The final part of this book discusses Kotter's eight-step process for change, explaining how to see change through to completion. Every time we don't complete a change, we break trust and create a little more resistance for future changes. So, always remember that it is our responsibility as Change Superheroes to model textbook change that builds trust and credibility.

Case study in brief: addressing a culture of bullying and harassment

Company info: NHS Trust; 3,500 people.

Background: this NHS Trust had recently been found to be failing by the Care Quality Commission (CQC). It had also been accused of having a culture of bullying and harassment. A new executive leadership team had been put in place with many conflicting priorities and needed to show progress in both performance and culture. The interim HR director (HRD) had presented a board paper on how to deal with the cultural aspects, which had been signed off by his peers. However, some covert comments from a couple of colleagues indicated a lack of clarity on the work and its benefits.

Action: the HRD announced his plans to pause the cultural initiative at the next executive meeting because he felt there were still concerns amongst his colleagues and he would be meeting with each of them individually to gain more input. He went on to meet with each individual and found little real resistance, more a lack of understanding about the importance of the cultural initiative and a touch of 'not-invented-here-itis'. The HRD gently coached his colleagues to appreciate the direct relationship between the cultural issues, organizational performance and of course the CQC rating, which helped them to get on board.

Result: the board began to act as one cohesive team. Change has been seen by the CQC and the Trust is now rated as good.

Quick recap on Cultural Challenges

- We need to be prepared to search out and address both covert and overt conflict during change.
- It is worth stepping back and considering the underlying cause of a Cultural Challenger in order to plan how to address it.
- Different tactics are appropriate for different situations.
- We may not win every battle.
- Don't be afraid to ask for help from others.

Online toolkit

The following free change resources can be downloaded via: www.changesuperhero.com

- 'How to Handle Conflict' questionnaire

PART III

Building a Change Master Plan

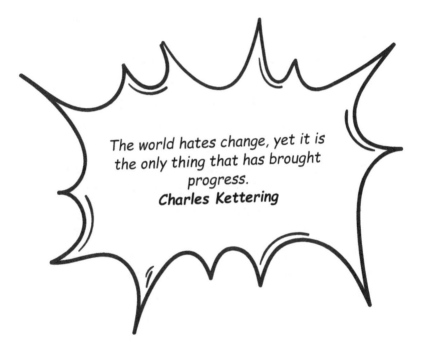

The world hates change, yet it is the only thing that has brought progress.
Charles Kettering

The above quotation illustrates the size of the task that many Change Superheroes have because 'the world' hates change, yet it has to be done if we are to make progress. The first two parts of the book have helped us to understand the key attributes of a Change Superhero and the obstacles that we may encounter on our change journey. We know what to expect from individuals during change in terms of emotions and personalities and have a good idea of the impact of different types of culture. We have lots of tools and tips that we can use to help us deal with engrained cultural issues and conflict. In short, we are in a pretty good place now to react to pretty much anything that change throws at us.

Therefore, this final part of the book will look at how we can 'do' change better, particularly large-scale change. Building on the insights and skills outlined in earlier chapters, here we will show you how to pull together your Change League of champions, ensuring the right skills are deployed at the right time and in the right place. We will highlight techniques and working models, such as Kotter's eight-step process, which can help you to plan for and deliver effective large-scale change. Then we consider our audience by emphasizing the importance of understanding who we are trying to reach and how to communicate convincingly with them. Finally, we reflect on the value of sharing this knowledge with others, expanding the quality and quantity of change skills in your organization, thereby increasing everyone's chances of success. Put simply, this part is about bringing all our know-how together and applying it practically.

CHAPTER 10

Build your Change League

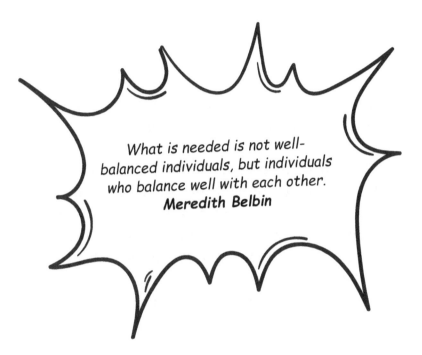

What is needed is not well-balanced individuals, but individuals who balance well with each other.
Meredith Belbin

The title of this book is *How to be a Change Superhero*, and by embracing even a handful of the behaviours and skills that we have discussed we can be pretty powerful agents of change. However, at the risk of overdoing the Superhero metaphor, we could be even more powerful by bringing together our very own Change League to deliver the change. Of course, this isn't really about gathering a breadth of Superpowers; instead, it is celebrating the power of a diverse team and Meredith Belbin's team-roles meta-phor is one of the best ways of understanding this.

We have already discussed many types of individual difference; however, the reality is that with every strength comes a natural blind spot. If we build our very own League of Change Champions then we can plan to embrace these differences and utilize the different strengths within our team at the optimum time. In Chapter 13 we walk through Kotter's eight-step change process and there are clear stages where certain skills are particularly useful.

The best-known model of successful teams was discovered by Meredith Belbin and his team in the 1960s and published in a book called *Management Teams* (Belbin, 2010). They noticed that people tended to take on certain behaviours and activities when they were in a team. Belbin grouped these into nine clusters of behaviour and called them 'team roles', defined as 'a tendency to behave, contribute and interrelate with others in a particular way'. This research proposed that each team would need to have access to all nine behaviours in order to be high-performing, although not necessarily all at the same time.

Now, this might suggest that we need nine people to be an effective team, but this is not the case because most people have two or three team roles in which they are comfortable. As is the case with personality types, each role has its own strengths as well as what Belbin termed 'allowable weaknesses'. An allowable weakness is simply the natural downside or opposite of a strength. I find this term helpful when working with others because it makes it OK to be less good at some things than others.

However, the real beauty of the team-roles model is that it explains how different skills are useful at different stages of a project. We need to understand and appreciate the pros and cons of each role to be an effective team. This knowledge helps us to understand the cause of competition rather than collaboration in a team if we have too many people with the same preference for certain team roles.

By looking across the spread of roles on a project we can predict where we may succeed or fail based on the natural composition of the team. This gives us the option to bring in additional team members with the missing strengths or to ask someone already in the team to take on a certain role instead. As outlined earlier, most of us have two or three roles that we are naturally good at. We also will have two or three roles that are manageable for us to take on if we focus our energy in those areas. While we may never be as good at that role, or perhaps enjoy it as much, as someone who has it as a natural strength, having the awareness and intention to take it on for the benefit of the overall team can make a huge difference.

Now, as is the case with any personality tool, if you want to be precise about your own team's make-up then you can diagnose your team roles using a self-perception inventory, such as the one accessible at www.belbin.com. However, for the purpose of this chapter, all we really need to do is understand the theory of the nine different roles and when they are most useful. I have outlined them below in the order that they tend to be most useful within a project.

At the beginning of a change or project

Shaper

As the name suggests, this is quite a dominant role, usually filled by someone who is assertive, confident and outspoken. Shapers challenge the team to improve, deliver on time and provide a sense of urgency. They are good at getting started, overcoming obstacles and are goal-oriented. At the start of the change, there is often confusion; therefore, the shaper role is good at cutting through and steering a path.

Allowable weakness

A shaper's bluntness and goal orientation can be seen as argumentative and they may be accused of offending others or hurting their feelings. So, while they are good at the start of change, it is important that they utilize other, more people-orientated strengths like listening and empathy when communicating change to others.

Resource investigator

People with this strength are optimistic, enthusiastic and naturally collaborative. They are quick to act and great at exploring options and solutions or negotiating for resources. At the start of a project or change, their enthusiasm is contagious, making them skilled at winning over cynics and influencing stakeholders.

Allowable weakness

Once their initial enthusiasm wears off, the resource investigator can lose interest or get distracted by the next project. They may forget to finish things or overlook details.

Coordinator

While both the shaper and the resource investigator are good at getting a project started, they can be more individualistic. The coordinator is the one who takes on the traditional team-leader role, agreeing specific objectives, delegating tasks and guiding the team to achieve the desired outcome. They are calm and understand the individual strengths of each team member and, as the name suggests, are good at coordinating these strengths in pursuit of a key role.

Allowable weakness

Coordinators can sometimes be seen as manipulative or be resented for excessive delegation.

During the change or project

Implementer

These are the people who get things done; they turn ideas and concepts into action. They are practical, systematic and disciplined. They are reliable and well organized and can be counted on to follow the plan and achieve their goals. While implementers may need to be won over initially in response to a change, once on board they are highly loyal and committed.

Allowable weakness

Because they like to follow a plan, implementers can be seen as inflexible or uninspiring.

Teamworker

These are *people* people. They are harmonious and supportive and will work cooperatively with others in the best interests of the team. They tend to be flexible, diplomatic and good at reading the emotions of others. This makes them good communicators and they display high levels of empathy. Teamworkers are useful at all stages of a project because of their flexibility. However, they will tend to avoid the conflict that can arise at the start of a project when the more dominant styles compete for control. This means they fit well in the middle and towards the end of a project when individuals are comfortable in their roles.

Allowable weakness

Their desire to get on with others can make them shy away from conflict and they may seem indecisive or unwilling to take a clear position during team discussions.

Plant

This is the person who tends to be creative and full of ideas, although they can be introverted, so may need to be encouraged to share their thoughts. They are deep thinkers and good at solving complex problems. These skills can be useful at the start of a project when brainstorming initial ideas, or in the middle of a project when obstacles may have arisen. If involved in the project at the right stage by a coordinator and focused on the requirements of the change, they may foresee issues that others have missed.

Allowable weakness

They may be poor communicators or too quiet to speak up. Sometimes, their ideas may be impractical or too abstract to use.

Specialist

This team role was added later by Belbin, as originally he outlined just eight roles. The idea of the specialist is the role of technical expert and this may be required at any stage during a change. As alluded to in the following chapters, many changes can fail due to poor information-gathering during the planning stages. Bringing in a specialist at the right time can help to avoid this.

Allowable weakness

Because of their specialism, these individuals may appear hung up on technicalities or may be considered intimidating. Depending on their other team roles they can seem less committed to the overall team.

At the end of the change or project

Monitor evaluator

These people are great at analyzing and evaluating ideas that others have come up with and will often spot problems before they arise. Clearly, this skill makes them useful during a change or project, not just at the end. However, because they are critical thinkers and think hard before they act, they are often more visible towards the end of a project. They also have a keen eye for quality so come into their own when the shapers and resource investigators try to cut corners or lose interest. They are shrewd and objective and can prevent mistakes from arising.

Allowable weakness

Sometimes accused of 'analysis paralysis', they can get bogged down in small details or be accused of slowing things down.

Completer finisher

This is now a pretty well-known term and, as the name suggests, is the role that ensures the project is seen through to the end. They will dot the 'i's and cross the 't's and ensure that there have been no errors or omissions. They are very focused on meeting deadlines, so if a project has been well structured with regular milestones, they will also keep the team on track along the way. They are conscientious, orderly and thorough.

Allowable weakness

Because of the focus on perfectionism, this role may be seen as overly critical and a bit of a worrier.

So, although each role has been described rather like a person, it is important to remember that we are all able to take on any role if we choose, and we will all have at least two roles that come quite naturally to us. However, as is always the case with people, there are some roles that we are better at than others in certain situations. Therefore, it is always better to bring in someone with a natural strength rather than force someone to take on a role that they find difficult. In my experience, certain roles are very rarely found together as strengths in the same person, e.g., a resource investigator is rarely a completer finisher, probably because the natural strength of one is the allowable weakness of the other and hence they fit well at either end of a change project.

Combinations of roles within a certain person are interesting as well; someone who is a shaper as well as a resource investigator or teamworker may have their rough edges softened, making them less likely to offend. On the other hand, a shaper as an implementer or completer finisher could be a highly effective task master.

If you are setting up your own Change Team then I recommend that you share these roles with them. You can download a summary document from our online toolkit to help. This will allow you to explain the different roles in the team and when they are needed. People will naturally know their most and least preferred team role and this will give you the opportunity to consider whether to bring in additional team members and what roles they need to take on.

Remember to look for and celebrate differences here. We tend to be drawn to and like people who are similar to us, but that will not build a balanced team with good representation across all nine roles. Not only that; even if you are the most senior person in the team or the person officially tasked with leading the change, you don't have to take on the role of team leader if your natural strength isn't that of a coordinator. It is perfectly fine to give someone else the role of team leader for the purpose of delivering the project. Building a well-balanced team and allowing everyone to play to their strengths will result in a far better outcome than having a team of clones with people playing roles that are outside of their comfort zone.

The stages of building a high-performing team

Now you have identified the right people for your Change League, it is worth being aware of the different stages that each team goes through in the process of building towards high performance. Tuckman's team development theory (1965) explains this, often being referred to simply as: forming, storming, norming and performing. This describes the visible stages that teams go through before performing at the optimum level.

Forming

The team has been assembled (ideally with a good spread of Belbin team roles) and the task is allocated. At this stage there is no real sense of 'team', so although goodwill may exist, team members do not know each other well enough to unconditionally trust each other. If time is spent planning the task and getting to know each other, including natural team roles and allowable weaknesses, then this will set an excellent foundation to accelerate through the next, more challenging, stage of storming.

Storming

The team has started to focus on delivering against the task, generating different ideas and solutions. At this stage it is entirely natural for differences of opinion and conflict to arise. If the team is prepared for this and it is managed well then this is a powerful and bonding stage as the team resolves its differences and moves towards consensus. On the other hand, if conflict is allowed to become personal, get out of hand and/or is not resolved constructively the team may never trust one another and may become dysfunctional.

Norming

Assuming a positive outcome to the previous stage, then the team starts to move towards established processes and harmonious working practices. Each team member feels confident to take on their own role and deliver their part. As they become more established, build trust and continue to improve, the team reaches the optimum stage of performing.

Performing

This is a synergistic, high-trust level of teamwork where results are delivered and team members rely on each other and value their contribution. Unfortunately, some teams never reach the level of performing, probably due to meeting challenges along the way as the other stages can feel difficult. Again, awareness is the key to a smooth journey and transition from forming to performing.

Of course, team members leave and change projects are completed, so Tuckman added on additional phases known as adjourning and transforming to cover these stages. Others have also used the term 'reforming'.

Using and sharing our knowledge about the stages of team development and team roles can be a really effective way of setting our Change Team up for success. It is important to disseminate this knowledge so that our Change League can operate independently and set up other teams throughout the organization with equally positive chances of success.

Case study in brief: utilizing team roles when building project teams

Company info: telecommunications firm; 2,000 people.

Background: this was a fast-moving firm with multiple projects in progress at once. The difficulty was that the same people tended to be used time and again for projects because of their visibility to the board. This was impacting their ability to deliver in their own day jobs and meant that projects were dragging on or were not finishing.

Action: the head of learning and development proposed that all managers in the organization would carry out Belbin team-role profiling. When new project teams were set up team members with the appropriate technical skills would be selected first and the rest of the team would be resourced from the wider pool of managers based on their Belbin team roles.

Result: over the following 18 months, 50% more projects were completed on time than the previous year and the number of people involved in projects grew from 40 to 100.

Quick recap on building your Change League

- We all have two or three preferred team roles that will be effective at different phases of a project.
- Identify and value differences when building your Change League.
- Just because you are responsible for delivering the change, that doesn't mean you have to lead the team.
- Conflict is a natural and positive stage of building a high-performing team, if managed well.
- Sharing knowledge about team roles and stages will help you to deliver change more widely and effectively.

Online toolkit

The following free change resources can be downloaded via: www.changesuperhero.com

- Belbin team roles summary

CHAPTER 11

Planning large-scale change

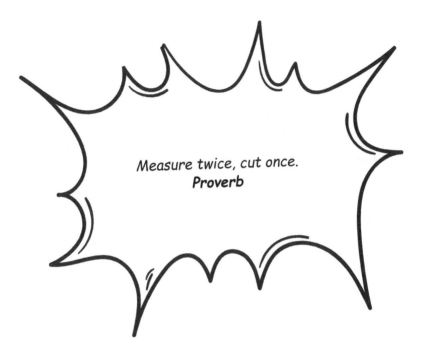

Measure twice, cut once.
Proverb

As Change Agents we are quite often brought in to manage or deliver a change that has been decided upon by others. Sometimes we are given the freedom to find the solution to a specific business problem and manage the change at our own pace. However, rather too often the Change Agent is presented with a *fait accompli*, including expectations and desired time frames, which may not always be realistic. The first thing we need to do when presented with our Change Challenge is to establish the facts, not least because they will form the foundation of our Communication Plan, which is outlined in the next chapter. The following seven steps form an invaluable structure to fact-find before planning our change.

Establishing the facts is about understanding what is involved and what the project aims to achieve. We need to know what is in or out of scope, timelines and who is involved. It is essentially about gathering all the information that is currently available about the change and capturing it in one place, ideally in one document. By defining the answers to a simple set of questions, we begin to build the information that we will need to build the Communication Plan and manage the change. Our seven fact-finding questions are outlined below, and you can download a helpful summary of these to help you plan your own change from the online toolkit. Our goal is to be ready to answer these questions clearly and succinctly on a couple of pages of A4.

- What is the change?
- Why do we need the change?
- What does success look like?
- How does this fit with other ongoing programmes and projects?
- What and who is in scope?
- How will the change take place?
- When is it happening?

What is the change?

Can we simply summarize what the change is in one or two sentences? So, we may have been brought in to support with a 'company restructure' or a 'systems refresh', which are general terms that can be appropriate in many circumstances but tend to raise a lot of questions too. Consider how the change can be explained more specifically – in one sentence, if needed. For instance, 'We are closing down our Newcastle site and relocating all staff to a new site in Middlesbrough' or 'We are moving from paper-based appraisal to an online performance and talent management system'.

We will use the second example to work through the rest of the fact-finding questions.

Why do we need the change?

What is the reason for the change? This is about understanding the evidence or business rationale for moving to an online performance tool and the consequences if change were not to take place. Consider the Change Equation that was discussed earlier in the book; we need to be able to create dissatisfaction with the status quo. Try to gather as many reasons for change as possible that will resonate with all levels of the organization and that are in keeping with the culture of the organization.

Example 1

We need to compete better in the marketplace; therefore, we must transform ourselves into a high-performing business with better alignment against objectives and better visibility of high and low performers.

Example 2

We need to increase retention of staff. Our staff survey told us that one reason people are leaving the business is because our current appraisal doesn't result in development or career opportunities. A new system would help us to develop and retain talent.

Example 3

Our paper-based HR systems present a compliance risk in terms of data protection and capturing and reporting on key regulatory requirements. An electronic system will help us capture and retain data securely as well as automatically alerting us to certification expiry dates. This will help protect us as a business.

Different reasons for a change will resonate with different audiences. Although we are just fact-finding at this stage, it is important that we can make the link between the change requirements, overall strategy and the individual. We can do this by continuing to ask or think 'why'; another way of doing this is by saying '… which means that'.

'Why' explains the rationale for choosing a certain point of action, creating urgency or a 'burning platform', e.g., 'we need to be more competitive in the marketplace'. Why? Because we are losing business to competitors and will lose jobs or go out of business within six months if we don't change now.

A more positive approach is using 'which means that', e.g., 'we have a high attrition rate, which means that we are losing talent faster than the competition, which means that we are less able to innovate and compete, which means that we could go out of business within six months if we don't change now'.

What does success look like?

Do we know what the vision of success is? This needs to be specific and tangible with goals and milestones that can be used as measures of success. While we may have big visions of beating the competition or reducing attrition, it can often feel quite vague or general for those directly impacted by the change. Where possible we should attach metrics to these to make sure that they are tangible and use SMART goals, as discussed earlier.

So, we may want to state that the overall goal is to: reduce unforced attrition from 16% to below 10% by XYZ date, or to achieve gold status in our external data protection assessment by ABC date. These overall goals support the vision; however, they are likely to be affected by a number of variables, not just the new system that we are introducing. So, we will also need some specific success measures for our actual project or change and they need to be shorter-term. In Chapter 13 we examine Kotter's eight-step process for change. A key part of this process is the ability to celebrate the first 'quick wins' of the change to encourage people to keep pushing through. What do we think those quick wins could be? It is important to define tangible success measures along the way (again, like SMART objectives) that give us something to aim for, to show we are on track and to keep people focused and motivated.

Let us continue with our earlier example of moving from a paper-based appraisal to an online system. This is very often an annual process, or at best six-monthly, so what indicators would provide evidence that change is happening over the short term? Examples might be: the average number of objectives people have put in the system; the frequency of logging into the system over the first three months; or the average number of one-to-ones recorded per person in that time period. We need to set short-term metrics and goals that we can track because these will provide evidence as to whether the wider behaviours of the organization are changing. We know that telling people once or twice to do something new is highly unlikely to result in change, particularly when it involves behaviour or culture change and it isn't perceived to be a life-or-death issue. Remember, we indicate what is important by what we measure consistently, so we must put some success measures in on the way to the vision. Clearly, there must also be consequences aligned to these success measures, so the department that has 100% staff with three objectives or more in the system within the first six weeks should be held up as a role model and recognized. On the other hand, the department or manager who clearly hasn't engaged at all with the new system needs to be taken aside and challenged, ideally with support from senior sponsors.

The interesting thing here is that with this project, the overall vision is most likely to be achieved through culture change – managers carrying out better performance management activities on a regular basis, using the software system as a catalyst. However, we know that focusing purely on culture change doesn't necessarily work. So, by breaking down the vision into tangible activities that can be reinforced we start to change the culture. Once the new activities are happening, we can then focus on the quality of these activities. As long as we recognize those 'quick wins', particularly from those who are also modelling the right culture and values, in time we will look back and recognize a cultural sea change has taken place.

How does this fit with other ongoing programmes and projects?

This is a practical question, which is often overlooked. For example, do you need lots of HR or IT resource to roll out your initiative or is there something else already scheduled that could distract or derail your programme? I have lost count of the number of times that I have seen excited Change Teams invest hundreds of hours researching, scoping and planning a project only for it to be pulled at the last minute because it might clash with another initiative that they were unaware of. It is particularly common in hierarchical cultures where the planning of the project is delegated but the senior stakeholder takes no notice until it comes to signing off the contract. It is only then that they think of the broader ramifications and may pull the plug at the last minute. This is such a waste of resources and demoralizing for those involved so it is worth asking this question as early as possible. Occasionally, it is unavoidable, for example, when the parent company announces a takeover or merger that no one knew about. However, all too often this could have been avoided by ensuring that the project was properly sponsored in the first place and that this sponsorship includes the final decision-maker.

What and who is in scope?

Back to our project, now we need to consider what exactly is involved and who it will affect. This is 'scoping' the project to decide on its size and it is important to avoid 'scope creep' where the project becomes too large and uncontrollable and outgrows the original timescale and budget.

There is a definite parallel between all these exercises and project management skills, which are well worth developing as Change Agents. Again, to avoid last-minute issues we should gather information from key sponsors to ensure that the scope of the exercise is agreed and well understood. Often, it's only during the scoping exercise that we start to realize some of the challenges that haven't been factored into the schedule. This allows us to set a more realistic target or timescale. Even with large-scale change it is wise to break the changes down into small chunks, allowing us to complete and consolidate each activity before starting again.

Continuing with our earlier example, this might mean that we decide to focus on rolling out the core performance management functionality in year one and will embed it within the whole business before moving on to incorporate talent management or 360 feedback. On the other hand, we might choose to roll full functionality out to a particular audience, perhaps as a pilot or a staggered roll-out. Either option has benefits and there are variations in between.

How will the change take place?

There are lots of ways to roll out change. Here are four options to consider.

The 'Big Bang' approach

If we are trying to achieve culture change, it can be easier to go for the first option, sometimes known as the 'Big Bang' approach. We might set the milestones lower but involve a wider audience. This enables us to support the roll-out with company-wide messages that support the change. In this situation we are more likely to get involvement from senior sponsors and the visibility of the project will be greater. It also means that we can recognize quick wins and enforce consequences at organizational level because we have been very clear about the overall behaviours and expectations.

However, if we are aiming to move a large organization forward in this way, it is important to be realistic about time frames and the complexity of the project. Generally, it is better to start simple and add functionality or complexity over time. Depending on the size of an organization it's important to be realistic about how long any type of change is going to take. My recommendation would be to allow at least three years to achieve culture change, hence the importance of short-term success indicators along the way. This is also why you may need to refresh your Change Team after year one, for example.

Pilot

A pilot is a small-scale roll-out of a new system or process to assess the suitability before a wider roll-out. Very often a pilot is the preferred route for the risk-averse organization; however, the difficulty is that this type of organization is also likely to have a traditional culture that resists change. In some environments, simply using the term pilot may signal that it is an optional change that can be resisted or pushed back on, setting it up for failure.

If we still feel that a pilot is the best starting point, we just need to recognize that it can also be full of challenges and should be approached with caution. Start by understanding why you want to run the pilot; what is the purpose? How long would it be for and what are the success measures? What is the audience? Can you see that to run a successful pilot you need to ask all the questions that you ask of a full-scale change?

We could say that the pilot is simply there to demonstrate that a system works, is user-friendly and can be configured to meet our needs. The issue with all of these requirements is that there is a significant investment in resources and time to evidence any of the outcomes. Effectively you and the provider will need to invest the same amount of time in setting up the system or project for a small short-term pilot as you would for a full-scale roll-out.

The other thorny issue is deciding who to include in the pilot. In principle, we want it to be a success and a platform from which to launch a full roll-out. So, do we start with the naturally more resistant audience on the premise that if we get them on board, we can get anyone on board? The risk is that they could undermine the whole initiative if they don't get behind it. Alternatively, we could start with a friendly audience who will be more supportive but perhaps less credible in the eyes of the rest of the organization when we move to a full roll-out. Perhaps a mixture of both? These are all questions that we need to consider.

As mentioned earlier, we are often requested to run a pilot in order to minimize risk. If that is the case, then one of the two following alternatives could be better options.

Proof of concept

This works well with software or professional services like training. If we are involving external parties, then we may have selected a preferred supplier, or we could be working with an internal team. The point is that there is an intent to work in partnership; however, we need certainty that the solution will work well within our environment. There may be a nominal financial investment to indicate commitment if we are working with an external third party, but contractual commitment to a large-scale roll-out has not been made yet. Once we have a proof of concept in the form of a system set-up or training outline, we can then involve a small group of people representative of the overall organization who can engage constructively with the system or service and provide feedback. The purpose is not to say yes or no to the system or solution, it is to provide tweaks and refinements that will improve the fit and support the roll-out. Those involved in the proof-of-concept evaluation may be ideal champions for the future roll-out. It also gives us a great indication of what the external company is like to work with.

Phased roll-out

You could call this a pilot in disguise – just don't use the word pilot because it can give permission for resistance. By calling it a phased roll-out, we are signalling that this change is here to stay. It is just a matter of timing as to when it will affect everyone. For phase one we should select a representative group of people who are likely to be keen and constructive. I have heard these termed 'early adopters' in one organization, which was positively received. There should be kudos attached to being part of this group as they have responsibility and influence by providing feedback on how future phases can be even better. Just this difference in terminology prevents obstacles being thrown up from those who just want to avoid change. Instead, it sets a scene of constructive problem-solving. We want to plan for our change to succeed and pre-empt obstacles, rather than creating room for doubt by using the term pilot.

So, we have decided what's in scope, who is in scope and whether it is to be a 'Big Bang' or staggered roll-out. We then need to set the specific goals and outcomes and consider our timelines.

When is it happening?

Having scoped the project, audience and roll-out plan we can start to consider realistic time frames. Unfortunately, all too often we are brought in to roll out a project where the only thing that has been defined is the vision and the time frame. In an ideal world we would be brought in early enough to scope the project and base the time frames on that information, yet frequently this happens back to front. More time spent planning will almost certainly shorten the implementation timelines as concerns and issues can be spotted in advance, messaging adjusted and diaries managed.

Ideally, we wouldn't rush the planning stage; however, it can be good to have a sense of urgency around a well scoped and planned project, as people lose momentum when a change is too drawn out. I would suggest that many changes are best being managed in 6 to 12-week blocks. Think of this as going from 'unfreeze' through to 'refreeze' in that time frame (see Chapter 13) or to at least have achieved several milestones or quick wins before moving onto the second phase of a project. Very often the execution of a project can be naturally broken into phases of this length.

Conclusion

In conclusion, if you know you are likely to be involved in managing a change project, try to get in early enough to ensure that you don't get landed with unreasonable time frames that drive the project and affect your ability to deliver quality.

Case study in brief: proof-of-concept system roll-out

Company info: financial services business; 50 people.

Background: a small, cautious firm with a handful of HR systems in place, requiring a compliance solution to meet the requirements of its financial services regulator. The regulatory changes impact those with both compliance and HR responsibilities.

Situation: the firm identified a provider with a compliance solution; this also had some HR functionality that would overlap with existing systems. It liked the idea of a 'one-stop shop' for its HRIS and compliance requirements but was nervous about removing an established system.

Action: for a small fee, the software provider set up a proof-of-concept version of the entire system and a small working group was able to comprehensively test all aspects of the functionality without giving notice on the firm's existing systems.

Result: after three months the firm felt confident that the new system could provide a comprehensive and more cost-effective solution and signed the contract. The implementation time was drastically reduced because the firm already had a configured system and was familiar with it and ready to go. It also reduced its HRIS spend by 30%.

Quick recap on planning large-scale change

- Consider how to message the change in a way that appeals to different audiences.
- Involve sponsors early to ensure visibility of potentially conflicting projects.
- Define milestones and deliverables that can measure the project progress and recognize 'quick wins'.
- Be cautious about the term 'pilot'; can the same outcome be achieved through a different route?
- Try to get involved as early in a change as possible to ensure realistic time frames.

Online toolkit

The following free change resources can be downloaded via: www.changesuperhero.com
- '7 Steps to Plan Change' template

CHAPTER 12

Building the Communication Plan

Most companies under-communicate their visions for change by at least a factor of ten.
John Kotter

As outlined in the previous chapter, if we have been brought in to design and manage the communication for a change, then ideally we would also have been involved in scoping the change. This would put us in a strong position to devise the Communication Plan. Unfortunately, all too often, communication isn't considered until change is well underway, often as a response to what is perceived as large-scale resistance. Of course, we now understand this resistance is simply the natural reaction of people experiencing the Change Curve *en masse* and it is to be expected, particularly without adequate communication up front. The problem is that it results in those delivering change feeling ambushed with questions to which they don't have the answers.

Ideally, communication should be well thought-through and planned before the change starts, as it can smooth the process significantly. Good, proactive communication can overcome resistance and help individuals buy in to change before it is even necessary. It reduces the emotional toll on those delivering and affected by the change and it gives the Change Team time to consider implications of the change that hadn't previously been considered.

How long ahead should we start communicating? Well, this depends on the size and scale of the change. Starting to plan three months ahead and rolling out the actual communications six weeks in advance would be a good guideline to work to for a large-scale change. Unfortunately, many of us have been saddled with the role of communicating change when it has already started. This forces us to be reactive and we can feel pushed into the position of damage limitation as opposed to positive communication. We should always try to go through the same thinking process about our Communication Plan, wherever and whenever we begin.

Kotter tells us that we need to communicate change ten times harder and more frequently than we think we need to. We know that communication is often the missing ingredient that can take us from 'freeze' to 'change' and back again. We have talked about individual communication and communication styles, but we haven't yet looked at large-scale communication, which is so important during transformation yet very often overlooked and/or under-resourced.

In this chapter we are going to consider how we could put together a large-scale Communication Plan, the different types of message and media that we can use and a number of examples and templates within the online toolkit that you can use to build a Communication Plan for your own change programme.

There are four stages that we should go through when developing a Communication Plan.

- Understanding our audience.
- Defining key messages.
- Choosing a variety of methods to communicate.
- Refining communications in line with feedback.

Understanding our audience

In other chapters we have discussed universal reactions to change, such as the Change Curve. We have also considered personality in relation to change. All these aspects are still relevant; however, when considering our audience we should consider people's relationship to the change in terms of their role as well as their levels of impact, influence and power in addition to individual personality. Using the term 'stakeholder' is a way of explaining the extent to which someone is affected by and/or can affect the change in question. We can use a stakeholder analysis to consider all the different types of people or stakeholders inside or outside the organization who are likely to be affected by the project or change. We can go on to consider what their possible response to the project or change is likely to be and whether they are most likely to be supporters or blockers. As we know, a few people (or stakeholders) can cause a project to succeed or fail.

During organizational change it is fairly obvious that it is important to first consider the impact on employees and managers, and there can be a whole subset of internal analysis in relation to the specific types of internal role or department that may be involved. However, some changes also require us to consider wider stakeholders such as customers, suppliers, trade unions or regulatory bodies. Some may be affected by the change and others may be able to impact the change; either way, they are still stakeholders.

Some initial questions to ask about stakeholders are as follows.

- Who will be directly/indirectly impacted by this change?
- How severe is the impact?
- Are they likely to perceive this as positive or negative change?
- How much power do they have as a group or individual?
- How much interest will they have in the change?

The four-box model below (Table 12.1) can be helpful for categorizing our stakeholders and means we can use this categorization to inform our Communication Plan. The two axes are power and interest, which results in four categories: high power with high interest, high power with low interest, low power with high interest and low power with low interest.

Table 12.1

Low power with high interest (vocalizers)	High power with high interest (key players)
Low power with low interest (peripherals)	High power with low interest (latents)

Key players

Stakeholders with high power and high interest can make or break a change so their buy-in is important. Therefore, they need to be involved from the start and it may be beneficial to have a one-to-one communications channel open with them, potentially ahead of the wider communications. It can be important to get them to act as a sponsor by putting their name to key communications or involve them in refining key messages.

Latents

Stakeholders with high power and low interest should be kept informed and again it may be worth having a personal conversation with them up front. Although they may have low levels of interest, they can scupper a change at the last minute if kept out of the loop. It may even be possible to gain their interest and subsequently move them into the key player space. By involving them in the early stages of change we can gain their commitment to support the project and check that they are not aware of any competing demands on resources.

Vocalizers

Stakeholders with low power and high interest need to be kept well informed. They need to feel involved and consulted to maximize the chances of buy-in. Although they don't have high power, they can come together as a collective to support or resist the change. Therefore, the communications should be positive and frequent, although this could be via video or email rather than one-to-one. With large-scale change, it is useful to have local Change Champions who can manage these stakeholders, helping them to feel supported without using up central Change Team resource.

Peripherals

Stakeholders with low power and low interest require less effort than the rest. They may just be informed of the change and any likely impact on them. Things can change, so it is worth monitoring them lightly.

Obviously, these are broad and blunt classifications, so it is important as a change manager to keep an eye on each stakeholder's requirements as the change progresses because their power status may change.

Defining key messages

In the last chapter we talked about scoping and fact-finding, which included defining our change project clearly – in one or two sentences. It also involved the ability to explain why the change is necessary. As you would expect, both pieces of information are highly relevant for our Communication Plan. We need to consider which information is most relevant and/or motivational and therefore likely to encourage each set of stakeholders, whether internal or external, to buy in to the change. When we think about it, it is obvious that trade unions will have different views from senior managers who will have different views from any relevant government body. Therefore, when we are building our Communication Plan, we need to be prepared to tailor our communications to cater to these different perspectives. This isn't about misleading people; it is about considering the change from their perspective and understanding what is most likely to be important to them. It is about focusing on the reasons for change that are most compelling and likely to resonate with each audience, motivating them to buy in.

Another aspect of planning change communications in-volves considering what the likely objections to the change are going to be and pre-empting these where possible. Pre-empting objections is about answering the questions that are in people's heads before they ask them; again, the objections will vary with the views of the stakeholder groups. Pre-empting objections is a powerful way of influencing people because it demonstrates that you truly understand their unspoken needs.

There is a helpful model that can be used to structure this type of communication effectively, known as 4MAT. It was originally developed by Bernice McCarthy (1980) with reference to David Kolb's (1984) well-known learning styles. Essentially, 4MAT is based on the premise that people ask four different questions when taking in information: 'why?'; 'what?'; 'how?'; and 'what if?' We have already covered the 'why' and the 'what' to a large extent during our fact-finding. However, according to 4MAT we can make our communications even more effective for more people by also preparing to answer the 'how' and 'what if' questions.

We generally need to start by answering the 'why', because this provides the reason and motivation to change. 'What' questions will explain what the change is, probably to a level of detail that is relevant to each group of stakeholders. It is also helpful to explain 'what' will stay the same as part of our communications to help keep the perception of the impact of the change proportionate.

'How' questions are likely to be either practical or personal. Again, they will vary according to the stakeholder in question. People need to understand 'how' they will be involved in delivering the change, including what they will need to do as part of their role to support or facilitate the change. If they are also on the receiving end of the change, they need to know how they will personally be affected.

The 'what if' category is all about understanding the potential implications of us making the change or not. By doing this, we are answering the questions, or pre-empting the objections, that are often overlooked but are likely to be in the heads of 25% of our stakeholders. Ensuring that all four aspects of 4MAT are included in our planned communications means that they are likely to appeal to the maximum number of people.

Let's consider a couple of examples.

Example 1

The change

A manufacturing business needs to move people from shift-based working with overtime to annualized hours, which means that the hours they are required to work will vary from week to week and overtime will not be payable.

Why?

- The parent company is demanding cost savings to deliver greater profitability.
- The marketplace has become extremely competitive and margins are being cut.
- Annualized hours are common practice for other competitors.

What?

- Staff will move from working fixed shifts to a variable working week that will be adjusted in line with demand.
- Overtime will no longer be available.
- The trade unions have been consulted and are reluctantly supportive.

How?

- This will be implemented from 1 April.
- Specific consultation on individual contracts will be available throughout February.
- Salaries will be averaged out over 12 months to allow for fluctuations.

What if we do?

- We will save enough money to remain open in the UK.
- A proportion of this revenue will be re-invested into R&D on this site.
- We will be able to keep 100% of current manufacturing jobs.

What if we don't?

- The factory will continue to be loss-making.
- 30% of jobs will need to be cut within 18 months.
- A proportion of the factory will be relocated to China.

Example 2

The change

A higher-education institution wants to introduce an online personal development review (PDR) system and encourage more frequent performance conversations.

Why?

- This university has a strategic vision of significant growth and needs to have the right systems in place to deliver this.

- The higher-education marketplace is increasingly competitive for students.
- The staff survey recently highlighted that the current performance and development review (PDR) process is ineffective and is causing staff to leave.

What?

- We are introducing a new PDR system that is popular in other universities and will be used for all aspects of performance, development and career management.
- It has been configured to reflect a new, improved PDR process developed by key stakeholder focus groups.
- All staff will be expected to use the new system and process from September.

How?

- All managers will be trained in the system and process in September.
- Access to the system will be rolled out from department to department during September and October.
- The 2020/2021 appraisal process will be completed online.

What if we do?

- We will be able to use information in the system to identify and meet training needs earlier for all staff.
- We will be able to better manage and reward high and low performers.

- We will be able to present ourselves as a high-tech, visionary university to future staff and students.

What if we don't?

- We will continue to struggle to manage staff career development effectively.
- We may not attract enough students to achieve our vision.
- Our staff will continue to leave due to our lack of performance management and development.

In both examples above, I chose three bullets in each area for ease, but don't let this restrict you. Capture as many points as you can under each heading, and you can then use this as the basis for all communications. You may choose to put more detail in some types of communication than others, but the detail won't be wasted. We will shortly move on to consider the different types of communications that we might choose to develop. However, first let us ensure that our communications are as powerful as possible, and this means we need to utilize the Change Agent Superpowers that we discussed in the first part of the book. In Chapter 3 on corroboration we talked about Cialdini's influencing styles and in the chapter on communication we discussed differences in how people like to take information in. We need to integrate this thinking when we are building our Communication Plan.

What do I mean by this? Well, in my experience a lot of corporate change communication is logical but bland. It is rarely influential and compelling, yet with a little thought we can make it so much more powerful. If we refer back to Cialdini's influencing model, there were six types of influence: authority, consensus, consistency, liking, reciprocity and scarcity. How can we incorporate these into our earlier change examples?

- Authority is used when we refer to the parent company or the trade unions and we would benefit by introducing a reference to authority in the second example, although the social proof of another university using the system may work as an alternative.
- Consensus is alluded to in the second example by reference to the staff survey and involvement of stakeholders.
- Consistency is referred to in both examples as the changes are being applied consistently across the relevant stakeholder groups.
- Reciprocity or exchange is evident to a degree by the R&D investment being offered and the annual salary being averaged out to accommodate any fluctuations. In the PDR example there is the offer of development and career opportunities.
- Scarcity could be seen to be demonstrated by the threat of closure or job cuts in the first example or lack of ability to attract students in the second.
- Liking is generally down to rapport, which would be more evident in the delivery of the message than the wording.

So, both examples show some evidence of using Cialdini's model of influence and would be reasonably effective, but they could be bolstered with a little more thought. Other relevant models that we could consider are the meta-programs from Chapter 4 on communication. The 'what if we do?' and 'what if we don't?' aspects of the 4MAT model should appeal to those who are towards or away-motivated, respectively. This helps reinforce the importance of including this aspect into any communications that we design. From our MBTI understanding from Chapter 7 we understand that some people will want the big picture and others will need more specific detail. We also appreciate that people have different preferences for visual, auditory or kinaesthetic language.

The basic principle is that we are trying to design communications that are going to be effective for the maximum number of people. We will have our own preferences and blind spots, so referring back to these models is a great way of spotting and addressing any gaps.

Choosing a variety of methods to communicate

Having considered the written messaging, it is now worth focusing on the method of delivery and to be mindful of the fact that it is virtually impossible to overcommunicate a change. We need to think about the methods of communication and the potential media we can use. It is not surprising that change doesn't happen when simply sent out in an uninspiring email.

So, we can communicate in writing and email is of course an option. We should also consider options like posters, websites or webpages with FAQs. Perhaps we can involve marketing and develop a brand for our change along with themed items. Then there is face-to-face communication, which might be one-to-many at conferences, meetings or town halls or to small groups or even one-to-one. We might create PowerPoint presentations or videos that are inspirational or authoritative. Can we get key sponsors to create individual video clips or messages that can be sent out to people, or to create video clips of people adopting the change or sharing their views about it? Can we ask managers to discuss and share information at team meetings? How about audio files or creating a podcast that can be listened to, particularly by employees who travel a lot?

We should make use of social media to reinforce key messages and make full use of collaboration technologies that are available to us or over web meetings. The routes and methods of communication open to us increase all the time and we should use as many as we can.

However, as the Change Agent responsible for communications, we are planning the communications and not necessarily delivering them, so we need to find ways of ensuring that the communications are well shared by others. If we can get an influential sponsor to deliver a live kick-off or launch and video it, then we can be sure that the message is consistent. Consider arming your Change League with key message 'crib sheets' and give them the opportunity to practise and rehearse the change story so they can deliver it with authenticity.

Plan regular communication updates at every available opportunity; grab a slot at internal conferences, in team briefings and newsletters. Communicate the progress and the 'quick wins' widely and in the early stages deal with those who are not progressing with a quiet word.

If your change has board sponsorship, consider how you can provide them with monthly or quarterly information; ideally, make it visual and consider the use of statistics of take-up or league tables. There is no doubt that a healthy bit of competition between internal departments driven from the top can result in a flurry of communication from those with power and accelerate the success of your initiative. In conclusion, remember that communication does not automatically mean action when it comes to change. This is why Kotter believes we should communicate so much more than we think we need to. However, if we put thought and effort into the types of communications that we deliver and make them relevant and influential, then they are far more likely to have the desired impact.

Refining communications in line with feedback

So, we have defined and started to roll out our communication and we know that we need to continue to communicate more thoroughly and for longer than we might have otherwise. We have already alluded to Kotter a number of times in this book and our next and final chapter goes on to explain his eight-step process for change. As you would expect, communication figures a number of times in this process and we should ensure that we are creative with our methods of delivery while still being consistent with our message.

However, we should also be prepared to seek feedback along the way, to understand how the messaging is being received. Are there certain questions that are being asked that we haven't prepared answers for? Perhaps we can update our FAQs or Change Agent crib sheets to accommodate these or release a video responding to some of them. We could survey certain stakeholders or Change Agents to find out how well they understand or have bought into the messaging or change and again adapt accordingly.

We should be prepared to adapt or clarify our messaging if it is being misinterpreted or not being well understood. There will be occasions when the message is understood but isn't particularly palatable and is met with resistance. The temptation can be for us to want to withdraw to avoid conflict but this is when our ability to communicate clearly, consistently and with empathy is most important. We need to look for positives and early signs of success and be sure to share these with others to reinforce the behaviours of those who are changing. We may want to tweak messaging or stand firm, depending on the feedback that we receive. Continuing to communicate even after a change becomes 'business as usual' is the key to ensuring change becomes fully embedded and we don't slip back around the transition curve.

So now we have considered who, what and how we should plan and communicate change to be successful. Our next and concluding chapter will allow us to bring all this knowledge together by applying it to Kotter's eight-step process for change.

Case study in brief: bringing reluctant stakeholders on board

Company info: oil and gas corporation; 60,000 people.

Background: an international oil and gas business wanted to move away from spot bonuses to peer recognition with financial reward. Due to the size and diversity of the business there was significant resistance from certain stakeholders who were concerned that the scheme could be open to abuse.

Action: the planning stage was managed by a communications professional who engaged the whole Change Team in the stakeholder analysis. Given the size of the business they assigned stakeholder owners to key influencers and specific audiences who took ownership for properly understanding and addressing concerns. In order to address the concerns it was decided to release the new system in waves with the most concerned group last.

Result: by the time of the third wave, the concerned stakeholder was convinced that the programme wouldn't be abused and was being pressured by his function to roll the new process out to them. 150,000 awards were issued in the first year for a population of around 60,000 people and, one year on, a number of comments in the engagement survey cited this scheme as a key motivator.

Quick recap on building the Communication Plan

- Start by understanding key stakeholders and what they want to hear.
- Use the 4MAT structure to plan the communication.
- Incorporate all of our other Superpowers to maximize the power of our communications.
- Give the Change League the opportunity to practise the messages.
- Don't stop communicating in a wide and creative fashion until the change is embedded.

Online toolkit

The following free change resources can be downloaded via: www.changesuperhero.com

- Stakeholder analysis planner
- 4MAT communication planner

CHAPTER 13

The process of large-scale change

70% of change initiatives fail due to people issues.
McKinsey & Company

This is a compelling headline, usually attributed to the McKinsey & Company consulting firm almost 20 years ago, although there have been many similar claims since. Unfortunately, this statistic seems to have been repeated over the years, with little significant improvement. Respected industry commentators such as *Harvard Business Review* and *Forbes* magazine continue to reinforce the claim that large-scale change still isn't delivering the kind of value that it was put in place to achieve.

So why is this the case? John Kotter (1995) is a well-known expert on organizational change and transformation. He believes that many issues are caused by leaders and managers treating the change as an event rather than a process with several defined stages. This means that rushing a stage or even skipping one altogether is likely to reduce momentum or even derail the change.

In my experience, all too often a 'change initiative' involves little more than a couple of emails from senior managers, resulting in little or no effective change. When we understand the process of change as explained by Kotter, it clarifies the follow-up activities that are needed to actually deliver change.

Before we move on to Kotter's model, it is worth taking a few steps back to understand the work of psychologist Kurt Lewin (1951; see Figure 13.1). He is particularly well known for the concepts of 'force field analysis', explained below, and his change theory, a three-step approach to change explained using the terms 'unfreeze', 'change' and 'refreeze'. Essentially, Lewin's theory sets the scene for change to be considered a process rather than an event, because in order to make a change we have to first 'unfreeze' the status quo, make the actual 'change' and then reset or 'refreeze' the new way of doing things. If we don't complete this final refreezing stage then it is human nature to swing back to the old status quo.

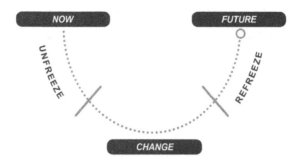

Figure 13.1 Lewin's change theory

Explaining why change fails

Anecdotally, these three stages are also particularly helpful in explaining why change fails, because it is often at a transition stage in this three-step model that change becomes derailed. Not only that – just like the McKinsey quote earlier, these problems are usually caused by people issues.

If we think for a moment about changes that we have been involved in that have failed or haven't been entirely successful in our organizations, it would be surprising if we were not thinking of commonly raised issues such as resistance to the new way of doing things, lack of sponsorship or resistance to buy-in. Other people-related reasons why change fails that regularly come up are:

- lack of buy-in/resistance to change
- lack of sponsorship/role-modelling
- lack of communication
- lack of sense of urgency
- lack of clear vision

- lack of impetus/follow-through
- lack of resources

So, what can we do about these blockers to change? Lewin's 'force field analysis' illustrates the fact that there are both driving and resisting forces in any situation that result in the current status quo. These forces could be people, processes or even habits or thoughts. Therefore, we will only be successful in achieving change if we have more driving forces than resisting ones. This may require creating additional driving forces such as communicating the change better, creating a clearer vision of the future, or by removing the key resistors, e.g., persuading people of the benefits of the change so that they become drivers rather than resistors.

This model is relevant for both individuals and organizations and, as can be seen in the example in Figures 13.2 and 13.3, the person in question is not going to achieve their current goal of being the perfect weight because the drivers and resistors are balancing out. They will be stuck with the status quo unless they can increase the driving forces and address the resistors. Dieting is a really simple but effective example because it also makes the point that you need to make permanent changes to your drivers or resistors – i.e., habit changes around eating – if you are not going to slip back to your old weight once the initial push for change is over. Of course, organizations are exactly the same; we may make a temporary change but the momentum of driving forces must be maintained long enough for new habits to be created if the change is to stick.

Think about a change in your organization. What are the drivers and resistors? This will help you come up with a strategy of who and what needs to be addressed if the change is to be successful.

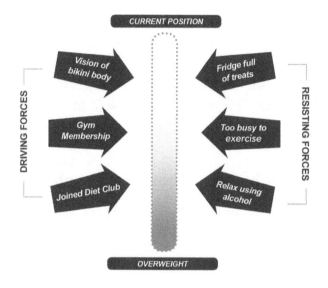

Figure 13.2 Lewin's force field analysis

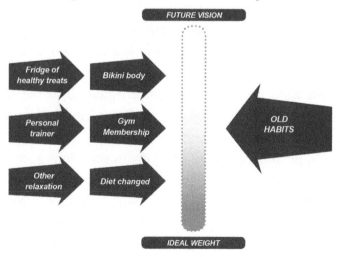

Figure 13.3 Lewin's force field analysis

So, both of Lewin's models of force field analysis and change theory provide a nice foundation for making change. However, it is John Kotter's eight-step process of change that really spells out the practical steps of making organizational change stick. This model was developed as a result of analysis carried out as part of his consulting practice with many different organizations that had gone through change. He converted this research into the well-known eight-step model that has been updated a few times over the years. This model is invaluable for both planning change and diagnosing why and where change has failed.

Kotter's eight-step process for change

This model outlines the different stages of the process.

Establish a sense of urgency

We may have heard or even used the term 'burning platform' to create an urgent reason for change. This powerful but unpleasant metaphor apparently stems from the Piper Alpha oil rig fire in 1988. Of course, very few of us would want to jump off an oil rig into the sea and would certainly prevaricate if there were no sense of urgency. However, if the oil rig platform were on fire then the decision is made for us; our lives are at stake so, of course, we will jump. Clearly, we don't want to push people into life-or-death situations in order to make change happen. However, it is a powerful concept – that establishing urgency around either moving away from danger (fire, in this case) or towards a positive future of safety (a lifeboat, in this case) will make change happen. The idea is that people will make even undesirable changes if they feel that the pain of staying the same is greater (remember the Change Equation discussed in Chapter 2).

We know that people are motivated towards positive outcomes and away from pain, and some of us are motivated more by one of these factors than the other. So, for us to motivate people to 'want' to change, we must consider the 'towards motivators', i.e., a positive future, and the 'dangers' of staying the same, in order to create a sense of urgency.

Form a powerful guiding coalition

The second stage of change is forming a powerful guiding coalition. This is likely to be our Change Team: a group of people who are going to work together to see the change through. We are at the stage of 'unfreezing' the organization now, so we should include senior sponsors as well as Change Agents or 'doers' at this stage. There are two points to note here; the first one is that the people in the guiding coalition do not have to remain the same throughout the change process; in fact, it may be advantageous to bring in different personalities and skills later. Second, we are likely to need more than one Change Team during large-scale change. So, we may start with a smaller steering group to define, plan and lead the change, and then expand this by engaging other champions or Change Teams who may be closer to the intended change and can ensure that any suggested plans are achievable.

Sometimes business change is decided behind 'closed doors' for good reasons – during an acquisition or restructuring, for example. However, for such change to be successful, it is likely that additional Change Agents will need to be brought in too, at some point, to help manage or implement the change. Unfortunately, system change in particular can be fraught with issues, if those who proposed it are not connected with the realities of implementing it within a specific time frame. This means that we would be wise to bring people in at the planning stage who have relevant specialist knowledge, even if they must be trusted to maintain confidentiality.

Create a compelling vision

Regardless of what the actual drivers of change are, this is where it is important for the Change Team to consider what the 'change story' is. It is likely to be connected to the burning platform concept outlined earlier but it generally needs to be positive, to motivate people towards a better future. People need to understand why the 'shiny new way' of doing things will be better than the current position. The vision needs to work on different levels or be translated into relevant motivators for different audiences at different levels within the organization. For example, shareholders may be motivated by share price but for employees job security or opportunities for development are likely to be more compelling as a future vision. This is about getting everyone involved in delivering the change 'on message' and it is worth considering what the likely questions and objections will be. This allows the guiding coalition to respond consistently and appropriately in line with the future vision.

Communicate the change

This is where the change starts to become real as we communicate in order to initiate it on a wider scale. This is one of the transition points between 'unfreezing' and 'changing' the organization and experience shows it is one of the first places that change frequently fails. Reasons for failure are plenty, including poor preparation during steps one to three, or people falling into the trap of considering change to be an event rather than a process, where simply telling people to change is considered enough. Add into the equation Kotter's argument that we need to communicate change ten times more than we think we need to, and it's easy to see why change commonly fails at this stage.

It is also important to consider that communication should be a two-way process. It is not enough to simply dictate change or expect it to happen as a result of a series of emails. As we know, with most change, people go through a series of emotions, which is where resistance commonly arises from. Communicating change effectively includes listening and responding to people's concerns and helping them to buy in and deal with any associated emotions around the change. Communication of change should take a variety of forms, including written and face-to-face, and it should use a variety of media to increase the chances of being received by all concerned. More on this point later.

Remove obstacles

This is where we need to start getting our hands dirty, and the success of this stage will be dependent on how well the change was planned in the first place. If we managed to build the right skills into the guiding coalition then their expertise will be highly relevant. Ideally, they will have already identified blockers that need addressing – remember the resistors in the force field analysis (see Figures 13.2 and 13.3)? This stage is all about getting rid of the obstacles that are pushing against the new way. Obstacles could be systems, structures or attitudes and behaviours. Addressing each will require different approaches and may take time. If we are introducing a new system, an obstacle may be the fact that people don't want to remember multiple passwords. A solution like single sign-on or password vault software may address this and needs consideration as part of the change. If the issue is around attitudes or behaviours then we need to talk to people to understand their objections and look to address them.

Create short-term wins

We are now moving back up the Change Curve into the refreeze section, and into another key transition where change can succeed or fail. Often, changes never even get to this stage – or, worse, a new change comes along, putting in place a new Change Curve that can result in worse overall performance, rather than better.

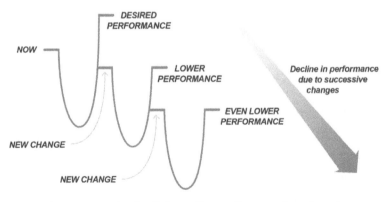

Figure 13.4 The declining effects of successive change

Looking for short-term wins and communicating these allows us to promote the success of the change programme. This is vital for numerous reasons; first, it motivates and recognizes those early adopters. Second, it clearly signals to those in denial that the change is real, and that it is here to stay. It is also important to start to demonstrate some of the benefits of the change and to help make the new way of doing things habitual.

Examples of quick wins could be announcing that 95% of staff have completed the required compliance e-learning by the deadline using the new learning management system (LMS), or in the case of a business merger we might announce the first business deal as a new commercial entity. This is a time for publicly recognizing those who have got on board with the change and privately nudging those who haven't.

This is also the time to consider bringing some new blood into your Change Team. Personalities suited to initiating change are rarely good at embedding it in detail. Implementing change is a different skill set to starting change. In Chapter 10 we talked about using Belbin's team roles when building the Change Team. We might select 'resource investigator' and 'shaper' types at the start of change but then move to 'implementers' and 'completer finishers' to push things through. Getting the right personalities in place at each stage of change maximizes our chances of driving things through into a 'refreeze' and ensuring value is derived from our change.

Consolidate improvements

Many organizations who go through mergers are held back by the legacy systems and processes that continually remind people of the old way. An example might be people who are still on old terms and conditions, making it difficult to embed a new recruitment policy, or old signage or headed paper. If the improvements are not consolidated it is incredibly hard to make sustained progress. The problem is sometimes that these aspects are overlooked; it almost resembles the Pareto principle – even though 80% of the change has been delivered, this last 20% of consolidation can make 80% of the difference in results.

You could see this like a succession of mini changes that have to be made to keep on consolidating the new way. It is important that the Change Team has the focus and enthusiasm to drive things through to completion at this stage.

Institutionalize the change

The final step, in Kotter's terms, is 'institutionalizing the new approach', although perhaps this sounds a bit dated. If we consider this to mean embedding the change, it is about ensuring all systems and processes are aligned with the new way of being. It is essentially building on step seven and taking it to completion. This is about the new way of becoming 'the way we do things around here'. In the case of a new recognition or benefits system, it might include new starters to the organization being inducted in the use of this as a cultural norm. It is only at this stage that we start to feel the benefits that we originally signed up to.

How many of the eight stages do you recognize in your organization? Overlaying Lewin's unfreeze-change-refreeze model onto Kotter's eight steps helps us to better understand the danger points where change breaks down. By understanding and sharing with others that change is a process not an event, we can appreciate the importance of seeing the change through to completion in order to reap the desired benefits. We need to be realistic about the requirements and challenges of each stage as well as the time involved in delivering large-scale change. If we follow Kotter's eight-step process consistently and enlist the different skills of our Change League as required, it is easy to see how we could gain greater, faster value from change in our organizations.

Case study in brief: utilizing Kotter's eight-step process to roll out a new performance management system

Company info: international medical devices company; 9,000 people.

Background: the company was getting ready for flotation and aspired to get into the FTSE 250 on launch (urgency). It wanted to demonstrate excellence in all aspects of its processes, including people management, and it wanted to demonstrate a structured approach to people and performance management (vision).

It procured performance management software and needed to embed it rapidly.

Situation: the company brought together HR business partners (guiding coalition) from all over the world to hear the vision from the CEO. However, a number of local obstacles became apparent such as language barriers and technology, all of which had to be overcome to achieve success (remove obstacles).

Action: the issues were resolved and wide-scale communication was delivered about the expectations of using the system (communication). The first goal of 90% of employees having three or more objectives set in the system was achieved within eight weeks of launch and widely communicated (celebrate quick wins). Further goals were set around development plans and appraisal systems were integrated and improved (consolidate improvements). The initial Change Team stepped back and an internal system owner was appointed with a keen eye for detail and a focus on embedding the system fully (institutionalize the change).

Result: 98% of development plans and appraisals were completed on time in that first year and in subsequent years this became business as usual.

Quick recap on the process of large-scale change

- To make change last it is important to 'refreeze' before moving onto the next change.
- We need more driving forces than resisting forces to create momentum for change.
- Communicating change does not mean it will actually happen.
- Many changes fail because steps 6–8 of Kotter's process are overlooked.
- It may be worth refreshing the Change Team towards the end of the process.

Online toolkit

The following free change resources can be downloaded via: www.changesuperhero.com
- Kotter case study PowerPoint

Conclusion

Change before you have to.
Jack Welch

It has become something of a cliché to state that change is all around us, but that doesn't make it any less true. Jack Welch tells us to change before we have to, to prevent us from getting left behind, and certainly 'doing' change rather than having it 'done' to us is likely to be preferable to most of us. The purpose of this book is to show that any one of us can be a Change Superhero. It is largely a question of choosing the right attitude and behaviours and understanding the needs of others. Then it is about us understanding the predictable process of change, applying common sense and good communication and being prepared to follow through.

Those of us who can adapt to change and help others to do the same can soften the human impact of change considerably. We can also increase the chances of the change delivering the intended results. It all starts with having the courage to stand up and be counted, coupled with the insight into the way others are motivated and how they process information. We can start small by understanding ourselves and then branch out, considering the preferences of our colleagues and the composition of our teams. A good way to begin is by reflecting on changes that we have experienced and evaluating what worked and what could have been improved. If you had been directly involved, what could you have done that would have made a difference?

Anyone can take the tools and knowledge in this book or available at www.changesuperhero.com and apply it successfully to their own environment. If you want more personalized support then you can check out one of our Change Superhero training courses or enlist one of our change consultants to build a personalized change programme in your organization. People find it reassuring to understand that the emotions they are feeling while going through change are completely normal and part of a natural process. Sharing models of team roles or personality preferences is a great way to engage with colleagues about individual differences and the impact this may have on the way we process change.

For those involved in planning or implementing change, using some of the tools in the final section, step back and consider the bigger picture around a change. It can help you to avoid some common errors like not driving the change through to completion or passive communication. We can all get involved in 'doing' change better; the question is, who will?

So, what have you got to lose? Harness your Superpowers, grab your cape and the support of your change colleagues. Remember: you too can be a true Change Superhero!

It may be hard for an egg to turn into a bird: it would be a jolly sight harder for it to learn to fly while remaining an egg.
C.S. Lewis

Online toolkit: summary

The following free change resources can be downloaded via: www.changesuperhero.com

- The 'Five Superpowers of a Change Superhero' quiz
- The 'Five Superpowers of a Change Superhero' infographic
- Influencing styles infographic
- NLP infographic
- 'Transition Curve' PowerPoint presentation
- MBTI and change overview
- Cultural Web template
- 'How to Handle Conflict' questionnaire
- Belbin team roles summary
- '7 Steps to Plan Change' template
- Stakeholder analysis planner
- 4MAT communication planner
- Kotter case study PowerPoint

Works cited

Bailey, R. (1979). https://labprofile20.com/. Accessed 17 February 2020.

Bass, B. M. (2005). *Transformational Leadership.* London: Psychology Press.

Beckhard, R. & Harris, R. T. (1987). *Organizational Transitions: Managing Complex Change.* Reading, MA: Addison-Wesley.

Belbin, M. (2010). *Management Teams* (3rd edn). Abingdon: Routledge. Retrieved from www.belbin.com

Burns, J. M. (2003). *Transforming Leadership.* New York: Grove Press.

Chan Kim, W. & Mauborgne, R. (2003). Tipping Point Leadership. *Harvard Business Review* (April 2003), 79–98.

Charvet, S. R. (1997). *Words that Change Minds* (2nd edn). Dubuque, IA: Kendall/Hunt Publishing Company.

Cialdini, R. B. (2006). *Influence: The Psychology of Persuasion.* New York: Harper Business.

Covey, S. (1989). *The 7 Habits of Highly Effective People.* New York: Simon and Schuster.

Goleman, D. (1996). *Emotional Intelligence: Why It Can Matter More than IQ.* London: Bloomsbury.

Hall, M. & Bodenhamer, B. G. (2006). *Figuring Out People.* Carmarthen: Crown House Publishing.

Handy, C. (1981). *Understanding Organizations.* London: Penguin.

Herold, D. M., Fedor, D. B., Caldwell, S. & Liu, Y. (2008). The Effects of Transformational and Change Leadership on Employees' Commitment to a Change: A Multilevel Study. *Journal of Applied Psychology, 93*(2), 346–357.

Higgs, M. & Rowland, D. (2011). What Does it Take to Implement Change Successfully? A Study of the Behaviors of Successful Change Leaders. *Journal of Applied Behavioral Science, 47*(3), 309–335.

Hofstede, G. (1994). The Business of International Business is Culture. *International Business Review, 3*(1), 1–14.

Johnson, G., Scholes, K. & Whittington, R. (1999). *Exploring Corporate Strategy.* Harlow: Prentice Hall.

Kanter, R. (2002). The Enduring Skills of Change Leaders. In F. Hesselbein & R. Johnston (eds), *On Leading Change*, pp. 47–61. San Francisco, CA: Jossey-Bass.

Kolb, D. (1984). *Experiential Learning.* New York: Prentice Hall.

Kotter, J. (1995). Leading Change: Why Transformation Efforts Fail. *Harvard Business Review, 73,* 59–67.

Kübler-Ross, E. (1969). *On Death and Dying* (Vol. 22). New York: Macmillan.

Lewin, K. (1951). *Field Theories in Social Science.* New York: Harper & Brothers.

Locke, E. & Latham, G. (1994). Goal-Setting Theory. In J. B. Miner (ed.), *Organizational Behaviour 1,* pp. 159–183. New York: Routledge.

Macpherson, C. (2017). *The Change Catalyst.* Chichester: John Wiley & Sons.

McCarthy, B. (1980). *The 4MAT System.* Boston: About Learning.

Meharabian, A. (1981). *Silent Messages: Implicit Communication of Emotions and Attitudes* (2nd edn). Belmont, CA: Wadsworth.

Myers, I. B. (1995). *Gifts Differing.* Mountain View, CA: Davies-Black.

Nohria, N. & Beer, M. (2000). Cracking the Code of Change. *Harvard Business Review,* May–June, 133–141.

Oreg, S., Vakola, M. & Armenakis, A. (2011). Change Recipients' Reactions to Organizational Change: A 60-Year Review of Quantitative Studies. *Journal of Applied Behavioural Science*, 47(4), 461–524.

Porter, L. & Tanner, S. J. (2003). *Assessing Business Excellence* (2nd edn). Oxford: Routledge.

Quinn, R. & Cameron, K. S. (2006). *Diagnosing and Changing Organizational Culture: Based on the Competing Values Framework.* New York: John Wiley & Sons.

Schein, E. H. (1984). Coming to a New Awareness of Organizational Culture. *Sloan Management Review*, 25(2), 3.

Schein, E. H. (2004). *Organizational Culture and Leadership.* London: Jossey-Bass.

Sivers, D. (2010). How to Start a Movement. *TED Talk.* Retrieved from www.ted.com/talks/derek_sivers_how_to_start_a_movement

Spencer-Oatey, H. & Franklin, P. (2009). *Intercultural Interaction: A Multidisciplinary Approach to Intercultural Communication.* London: Palgrave Macmillan.

Tuckman, B. (1965). Developmental Sequence in Small Groups. *Psychological Bulletin*, 63(6), 384–399.

Ugoani, J. N. N., Amu, C. U. & Kalu, E. O. (2015). Dimensions of Emotional Intelligence and Transformational

Leadership: A Correlation Analysis. *Independent Journal of Management & Production*, 6(2), 563–584.

Zhou, K. Z., Tse, K. T. & Li, J. J. (2006). Organizational Changes in Emerging Economies: Drivers and Consequences. *Journal of International Business Studies*, 37(2) pp. 248-263.